TRUE FREEDOM

A Revolutionary Approach
to Addiction Recovery

PART TWO

Partnering with the Truth

Divorcing the Illusionist

Rebekah S. Thomas

malcolm down

PUBLISHING

Endorsements

Reading through *True Freedom* made my heart leap with joy. It is extremely refreshing and revolutionary for recovery. Rebekah brings practical aids to our recovery and stories through which we can see our own lens emerge, providing a much needed pathway to journey out to lasting freedom.

I am convinced this new pathway for recovery will help any person struggling with addictive patterns of behaviour that can be hidden and cause repeated relapse. True Freedom brings what's hidden to the light where it can no longer have destructive power or influence in our lives. I highly recommend *True Freedom,* which can be run in a rehab or Church or one to one to heal a person's life.

Alison Fenning, RSVP Trust

In my 50+ years of ministry, I've worked with countless people who have been caught up in addiction. Bekah Thomas has written a fantastic guide that I believe will bring hope and purpose to many. *True Freedom* offers biblical, practical and incredibly wise counsel, which could be life transforming for many. She has not only provided great advice, but she has lived that advice, and in the book includes many examples of the lives she has seen changed. I pray this book will be a blessing to many.

Pastor Bill Wilson, Metro World Child.

Biblical, practical, clear and hopeful. This timely book will help many in their journey from addiction to freedom and I'm praying that it will be used widely and have a profound impact.

Gavin Calver, CEO, Evangelical Alliance.

The book is amazing. I LOVE it.

Like many other books this one deals with the science of addiction head on and how to break its destructive cycle. The psychology behind addiction is set out brilliantly. What makes this book unique, however, is that unapologetically it deals with recovery from addiction from a wholly Christian perspective. It sets out the hope of living free from its destruction, fear and self-loathing. It's realistic about the path of healing, outlining just how important the process is. Do you want to change? Do you know someone stuck in addition? Then read this book. I commend it highly.

Andrea Williams, Chief Executive, Christian Concern

I found Rebekah's take in *True Freedom* so refreshing and insightful. In many ways, a different angle from others, but one that works. I've seen this in the lives of many who pass through the Hope Centre.

Barry Woodward
Author of Once an Addict and CEO of Proclaim Trust

At the heart of all addiction is a pursuit. *True Freedom* is written with both passion and compassion. It is Spirit-led work that will bear much fruit. This is not a book to be read but a journey to engage with.

For many there is often a polarised choice between 12 steps or harm reduction, both of these - while proven and excellent often in practice – do not give a clarity to where truth and freedom is really found; this *True Freedom* work is abundantly clear.

Ian Mountford, Major
Corps Officer & Territorial Mission Enabler (THQ)*

I welcome this powerful and compelling book. Addiction robs people of their dignity and, ultimately, their destiny. From her experience helping people break free from life controlling addictions, Bekah offers in *True Freedom* a radical, hope filled and genuinely practical journey out of addiction into a new life of freedom and purpose.

Chris Cartwright, General Superintendent, Elim Penetecostal Churches.

I would consider Rebekah Thomas an expert on finding freedom from addiction, not just because of her personal story but also due to her many years of experience working with those who have struggled with addiction. I was so glad when I heard she took her years of experience and knowledge and put it into a book to help others. May this book encourage you, strengthen you, and help you to find true freedom.

Josh Hannah, Founder and President, Hope Center Ministries

True Freedom is a radical and carefully considered study, brought together through Rebekah's experience, learning and revelation. This is an exciting new approach that not only builds on former models but brings a new comprehensive dynamic to the understanding of what it means to experience and walk out True Freedom from addiction.

Trudy Makepeace, author, Abused. Addicted. Free.

Addiction is a curse that reaches beyond the user to affect everyone who feels its touch. What Rebekah has done is to map out a journey that, if followed, ends with release from the curse, and the start of a new journey of freedom. This really works – if you work it, and this book will benefit everyone who engages with it.

Rev. Paul Lloyd, Senior Pastor, Victory Outreach Manchester
VOI UK/Germany Regional Leader

I am honoured to recommend the *True Freedom* books by my friend, Rebekah Thomas. I have had the honour of seeing her work in Wales.

She lives out what she is teaching through this book. She pours her life into broken people day in and day out. Their organization is having a phenomenal impact on people on the pathway to freedom and healing.

Sujo John, Founder, YouCanFreeUs Foundation

First published 2022 by Malcolm Down Publishing Ltd.
www.malcolmdown.co.uk

25 24 23 22   7 6 5 4 3 2 1

British Library Cataloguing in Publication Data
A catalogue record for this book is available from the British Library.

ISBN 978-1-915046-40-6

Cover design by Angela Selfe
Illustrations on pages 127, 128, 129 & 130 by Danielle Lacovou

Printed in the UK

Disclaimer
This book is not a substitute for professional medical advice.
Readers are advised to see a GP if they are battling addiction.

Contents

'The thief comes only to steal and kill and destroy; I have come that they may have life, and have it to the full.'

John 10:10, the Bible

Introduction

I'm so glad that you've decided to continue this journey with me. If you haven't completed Part One, I highly recommend that you do so before reading Part Two, because all three parts constitute a journey from beginning to end.

I want to honour the addiction recovery models that have gone before this one. They have great value in many ways. However, the True Freedom model is a new and valuable tool. This approach to addiction recovery works for addiction in general: from nicotine to crack; from sugar to opioids; from a life-destroying cycle of torture to something coming between you and a person or goal that matters.

It will work for you whether you're in a residential rehab that uses True Freedom, part of a local True Freedom Community group, in a prison reading True Freedom during a group session or from your cell, journeying through it at home after work each day, or if a mentor, loved one or chaplain / pastor / leader is supporting you through it on a one-to-one basis.

If you have no choice but to engage with these workbooks alone that's OK, but I would highly recommend seeking out a mentor to oversee your journey if that's an option. Look for someone who loves you enough to be honest, even if it doesn't make them popular. Someone who is insightful enough to empathise with your brokenness, and who is a faithful, fruitful disciple of Jesus.

If you get confused, ask that trusted person to help you. If you have unwanted thoughts and feelings, ask them to pray with you. If you struggle to read and write, or to focus, ask them to agree to a time and place to go through the workbook with you. True Freedom Community Groups will be available on the website, and you will be able to view supported housing options where True Freedom principles are taught.

The True Freedom journey begins with three separate parts of the True Freedom workbook. You are currently holding Part Two. Part One unravels the deception that has kept you trapped, allowing you to move forward. Part Two unpacks the other forces at work in your life and in your addiction. Part Three leads us to take the action needed for addiction recovery to occur.

Each milestone ends with a statement of truth, which can be read aloud as a declaration of your progress. At the end of all three parts, you will have twelve milestone statements you can remember as keys to freedom, all of which are recorded at the back of this book.

Remember to visit www.truefreedom.com for more resources and ongoing support, which will also be helpful for anyone who wants to support you on your journey or start a True Freedom Community group. And don't forget to grab your journal or recorder so that whenever you see 📔 🎤 🎥 🔊, you can write, record or video yourself sharing what you've just learned in your own words, as if you're teaching it to someone else. If you have a mentor, friend or leader supporting you through this, read or play what you've recorded to them, and if you're part of a True Freedom group, share to teach each other what you've learned in your own words.

Much love,

Bekah

What other people are saying about True Freedom:

'It grips you before you realise it's about addiction, and then when the penny drops you're like, 'Wow, that's amazing!' It takes away the shame because now I know how addiction works.'
Debbie Greer

'When I started doing the milestones, it was like the author had been watching me; as if the milestones were tailor-made for me.'
Anthony Griffiths

'It's an outstanding piece of work, very interesting and insightful. Based on many years of addiction, I found this a simple and effective process, something I can carry into life.'
Mark Bailey

'Working through the True Freedom stuff is like finding the keys for a lock that no other place managed to help me find.'
Scott Warnock

'The milestones couldn't be more relevant. I thought I knew how things worked but I was wrong. I found the visual representation an eye-opener to what was actually happening to me.'
Craig Desmond

'When I picked up the workbook it blew me away – I thought it was aimed at me. This book will bring hope to others who are in despair.'
Charlotte Carradine

'This teaching helped me find true freedom from my addictions of alcohol and drugs of seventeen years. I tried other rehabs, counselling and recovery groups, and none of these worked for me. I am now actually living a life free from addiction, part of a local church community, marriage restored, running a Hope Centre and enjoying life free from addiction.'

Nicola Moseley (now employed in addiction recovery, using True Freedom material)

'I may have got clean without True Freedom, but I was not made well. True Freedom truly sets you free. It takes hold of so much recovery wisdom and becomes like a lens through which they make more sense.'

James Hackett (now employed in addiction recovery, using True Freedom material)

'It's just mind-blowing how you don't see it in the madness of living it, but True Freedom gives the light-bulb moment that sets you free.'

Lowri Marshall (now using the True Freedom material to lead addicts to the freedom she found)

PART TWO

Partnering with the Truth:
Divorcing the Illusionist

'The thief comes only to steal and kill and destroy; I have come that they may have life, and have it to the full.'

John 10:10

Debbie

There were no words to describe the heat. And the thirst? That was ridiculous! Debbie's lips were so dry and cracked they had bled until the blood dried and resealed the cracks. Her tongue was so swollen and sore she would have struggled to speak had there been anyone to speak to. Her mouth felt like the very desert in which she knelt. Her body was so dry that she was sobbing without tears, like a person so distraught they scream without sound.

Debbie had audibly screamed at first. She had screamed for help. She had screamed in frustration. She had even screamed at God. But all the screaming had done was exhaust her further. She wasn't screaming any more.

She had talked to herself at one point, but she hadn't the energy for that now either, and moving her tongue and lips was so painful. She had spent an unknown amount of time just lying on the sand feeling defeated, but she was back on her feet now. Walking, searching, hoping. Compulsively, instinctively looking for water.

How did I get here?

No matter how fruitless and self-punishing that internal question was, Debbie couldn't stop asking herself. Sure, she remembered the events that had led up to her desertion, but somehow that knowledge didn't seem to answer the question. She recalled her excitement about the holiday excursion. She had replayed the events of the first day towards this final destination over and over. She had analysed her decision to stray from the group and their decisions that led to losing her. And she had contemplated every alternative series of events. But none of this had made her any less lost, any less alone or any less likely to die from dehydration.

As Debbie reached the top of yet another mound of sand, she saw it. An oasis. She wasn't sure exactly how far away it was, but It looked to be about half a mile. It was within sight, and that's what mattered. It looked big as well. Debbie could see trees – healthy-looking trees, and lots of them – as well as birds flying over the area.

What amazed and excited Debbie most, however, was the presence of human life. *A village!*

Her legs had given in, and it had only been at that point on her knees that the oasis had become visible. It was also on her knees that she continued down the dune, almost allowing herself to roll down. Then Debbie dragged herself onto her feet, her eyes locked on the delightful sight, despite it being less visible from lower down.

'C'mon, Debbie,' she muttered to herself, her mouth tearing and her head exploding at every attempt to speak. 'One leg in front of the other. You can do it!' She gritted her teeth as she dragged her left foot in front of the right, and vice versa.

Suddenly, to her amazement, Debbie spotted a large puddle of water just a few yards to her left. A burst of adrenaline coursed through her veins, compelling her to run towards it. She fell forward into the water like a plank of timber, face-planting the puddle.

For a split second she enjoyed the feeling of liquid on her skin, but before she could stop to think, her mouth opened and her body guzzled the water so quickly that she inhaled some of it into her lungs. For a short moment it felt like the best experience of Debbie's life. A moment of indescribable joy and relief. The most instant and extreme gratification imaginable. But before Debbie knew it she was coughing and retching, her whole body convulsing uncontrollably as she rolled herself to one side of the puddle.

'Salt!' she cried out as she continued coughing, retching and convulsing. She was relieved to be coughing the liquid out of her lungs, but she knew that the salt in the water was of far greater concern.

By the time Debbie had thrown up all the bile her guts could muster, and had stopped convulsing, she remembered what she'd learned at school about salt water. She knew that her kidneys would be drawing water from her blood cells to filter out all the salt, making her more dehydrated than ever before. But now she was even more thirsty. And that guzzle had initially felt so good!

Debbie started to weigh up what appeared to be two options. She instinctively knew that she should recoil from the salt pan and put all her remaining energy into getting to the oasis, but she couldn't help thinking about how good that salt water had felt on her face and lips, and in her mouth and throat. Even the stinging sensation of the salt on her torn lips and tongue had felt oddly satisfying. She really wanted to feel that relief again. Just one more time.

Debbie rolled back over so her face was almost touching the salty water again. *Maybe if I just take a little sip, it'll relieve the thirst enough to give me the strength to walk to the oasis*, she convinced herself. Before her mind had a chance to refute the erroneous thought, she was sipping away at the water.

That's better. She breathed a sigh of relief. The small sip hadn't created the drastic after-effects of the initial guzzle. But her brain soon kicked in and reasoned within her, flagging the fact that any salt water consumption would only lead to further dehydration and make it even harder to get to the oasis.

But what if the oasis is just a mirage? Debbie asked herself in a thinly veiled attempt to justify staying where she was and drinking more salt water. *What if the oasis water is also salt water? Then I'll have walked all that way for no reason.*

She rolled her eyes, knowing that it was a silly thought, since she could see by the life around the oasis that it contained fresh water. Something deep within her yearned for that oasis; longed to find people who could help her, water pure enough to hydrate her and deep enough to swim in, food to eat and shelter from the harsh weather. Oh, how she desired that . . . and it was within reach. But she was so thirsty, and instant relief was right there for the taking.

Look how close the oasis is, she told herself, staring at the beautiful view once again. *But if it's that close, surely someone from the village will walk this way and save me before the dehydration kills me.* Her tongue began licking the surface of the puddle as she thought about it. Suddenly, she could resist no longer. Debbie dipped her face back into the water and gulped it down. Again, her body started to convulse, and she threw up what she had consumed. Tears filled her eyes, from where she couldn't fathom, as she curled up into a ball and pulled at her hair in frustration.

A split-second later, Debbie gave in to her desperation again, casting off all restraint and sipping from the puddle repeatedly. She knew not to take big gulps now, telling herself she was better off giving in and resolving to take constant, gentle sips than trying to fight it until she ended up guzzling. Debbie had become trapped in a vicious cycle in which the more she drank the thirstier she became, and the more she wanted to drink. Yet all the while she was losing the strength required to get to the pure water source that would save her.

She knew what she was doing was all wrong, but she blocked out the rational protests that filled her mind and focused all her attention on each fleeting moment of instant gratification.

Debbie lay on the sand, her face lying in the puddle, with almost all the energy drained from her body and her muscles cramping, her clothes wet with urine and her limbs unable to move. She forced her eyes open one last time. She saw the oasis in the near distance and imagined herself making a different choice when she had first discovered that the puddle was a salt pan. She pictured herself immediately rejecting the salt water and pressing on towards the oasis. She pictured herself swimming in the oasis pool, surrounded by fish and vegetation, with the trees offering shade and the people coming over to help her.

Then she drifted into a coma and died.

Milestone Six:

Escaping the Desert and
Embracing the Life-Changing
Oasis of God's Love

'The thief comes only to steal and kill and destroy; I have come that they may have life, and have it to the full.'

John 10:10

Salvation

We all find ourselves in some sort of desert at times in our lives. For some people, this desert is a specific struggle against the backdrop of a healthy and functional life. For others the desert is one trauma after another in a context of neglect, abandonment, rejection and abuse. In either case, God always provides an oasis: a place of salvation, healing, refreshing and sustenance for the soul.[1] Meanwhile, Satan – the illusionist – always provides a salt pan: a form of instant gratification that leads to further destruction. Salt water creates a vicious cycle, in which our kidneys use the water to flush out the salt, leaving the body increasingly dehydrated and yet increasingly thirsty. Just like addiction.

We don't always see as clearly as Debbie did that the salt water we are given is not good for us. Some people are never taught about the vicious cycle of instant gratification; in fact, we are sometimes overtly mistaught that the salt pan is good for us. Satan takes advantage of this unawareness and false teaching. There is not one person on this planet who is immune to the temptation of salt water in the desert. That salt water can become a vicious cycle of addiction to anyone, creating an ever-increasing need as it slowly kills us. Therefore, we are all potential addicts.

But how did we all end up lost in a desert to start with? God's story – the gospel – explains it all very clearly.

What do you think of when you hear the word 'gospel'? A genre of music? Something Christians talk about? Religion? Or God's story?

The word 'gospel' means 'good news', and the gospel of Jesus Christ is like the oasis in the desert. Some people who don't know God hear the word and associate it with bad things, partly because God's people haven't always told the story well over the centuries, but also because it's only good news for those who have understood the bad news first.

Before a doctor gives someone treatment, he or she must first tell the patient what's wrong with them. As such, even though the gospel is the good news of Jesus, the Bible tells a far bigger story that diagnoses the problem and explains why we need Jesus.[2] Funnily enough, many people assume they know this story, even though they've never read or heard it first-hand. I've been reading and hearing the story for many years, yet I still keep learning new details. Want to hear a bitesize version now? OK, then let's go back to the beginning, where all the best stories start.

The Importance of Community

Right from the start of God's story, we learn something important about his identity, because he refers to himself as 'us'.[3] This points to what we call the Trinity, where God is Father, Son and Spirit, three in one. This is a lot to wrap our heads around, but it'll be helpful to bear in mind for later. For now, we'll just focus on the fact that it demonstrates the relational nature of God, as does his choice to create.

I'm sure you've heard of Adam and Eve. If not, they were the first humans created by God, as recorded in the Bible. God made Adam, then said it wasn't good for him to be alone, so he made Eve. God wasn't caught off guard by Adam's need for companionship. He wasn't surprised by any sort of oversight on his part. God made one human alone at the start to give us this message. He wanted us to know that even in a perfect context with him, we need community.[4]

Can you recall an early memory of deep loneliness? How did it feel?

....

....

....

Sometimes we choose loneliness because being alone can feel more comfortable when we're ashamed or scared, but it's not good for us. Have you ever tried to stay completely alone, rejecting the idea of community and pushing people away? What effect has that had on your life?

....

....

....

>>>

The way God created Adam and Eve also tells us something. God made Adam and Eve in his image (which we'll come back to properly in Milestone Nine). Humanity is made up of three things: the dirt of the earth, the breath of God, and one another. While Eve came from Adam's body, every subsequent human has come from a woman. And through all of humanity runs the soil of the created and the breath of the Creator.[5] This is God's way of showing us that we are only complete when our lives are lived in harmony with creation, the Creator and one another. We were created out of creation, which keeps us humble. Our life comes from the life of God, which keeps us secure. And every man and woman since Eve has been a product of man and woman, which keeps us interconnected.

What do you recognise about yourself as being from the dirt (for example, mortality, inferiority, dependence)?

....

....

....

....

What do you recognise as being created in God's image – alive with his life, in a way that goes beyond this earth?

....

....

....

....

What do you recognise in terms of being intrinsically interconnected with humanity? Has that been a good or a bad experience?

....

....

....

>> >> >>

When God created Eve, he called her Adam's *ezer kenegdo*, which means 'helper', ' rescuer' or 'strength alongside'.[6] The word *ezer* is used on approximately twenty other occasions in the Old Testament. A few of these mentions refer to nations from whom the Israelites sought military aid but the majority refer to God rescuing the Israelites from their troubles.[7] God intentionally adds *kenegdo* in this instance because he wants to send us another crucial message. He wants to assure us that Eve is not greater than Adam, the way that God is greater than Israel, but that she is alongside him. Again, God has not been caught off guard here. He doesn't create Eve as a rescuer in place of himself; he creates her as a peer, with both in equal need of God. He very intentionally creates a team, a partnership. Adam and Eve didn't need to be greater than each other because they had God for that. They needed to be partners.

We all search for rescuers from our addiction, and we are designed to need and support each other. But only God is *ezer* above us.

Have you ever regarded someone as greater than yourself because they rescued you – allowing them to fill God's spot as your rescuer? Who was it? How did it turn out?

....

....

....

On the flipside to *putting others above us* to rescue us from our addiction, we sometimes *put ourselves above others*, giving us a sense of superiority to counter our sense of worthlessness and our feelings of shame. This is especially true when we live with addictions that society frowns upon, which adds to the shame. Sometimes people try to combat that inferior feeling by making others feel even more inferior. We try to place others lower than ourselves so we don't feel as low. This is why discrimination is common in situations of addiction. In short, we sometimes feel better about ourselves by looking down on others.

Have you ever leaned on a false sense of superiority over other people to make yourself feel better? How did that go?

....

....

....

Good Versus Evil

God partly made Adam and Eve as a display of his relational nature, demonstrating his love for community and collaboration. But what does the environment he chose tell us about God? He placed them in the Garden of Eden, in a perfect paradise. This tells us where we really belong. He is a generous God who wants us to be surrounded by goodness and his glory. That's what we were created to experience. Perhaps this is why we create, watch and read so much film and fiction about utopia, or about finding completion in a person or project. Is it any wonder that we seek to escape from the evil, monotony and emptiness we were never created to endure? Is it any wonder that we end up being tricked by the lie of addiction, precisely because our souls don't belong outside paradise?[8]

What thoughts and feelings arise as you ponder God's message that we belong in a paradise he wants us to enjoy?

....

....

....

What have you used to escape the darkness you don't belong in, or to reach for your own version of paradise?

....

....

....

Adam and Eve knew no shame, fear, angst or loneliness. They experienced good but didn't know it as 'good'; they just knew it as their reality, their norm. They didn't know that good was good because they had no knowledge of evil with which to contrast it. This tells us that God intended us for good – to be good and to live full lives – but it also provides us with a silver lining, because the more evil we've known, the more we'll appreciate and enjoy the good that comes when we place our future in God's hands. If you have access to a CD player or a music app, I recommend having a listen to 'Maybe It's OK' by Christian band We Are Messengers.

Adam and Eve didn't know what good was because they'd had no experience of evil, so good was just the assumed norm. Some of us can empathise with this – only, we understand this lack of knowledge in reverse, because we didn't know good. Some of us thought our dysfunctional childhoods were normal because that was all we knew. We didn't realise something was wrong until we spent time at a friend's house, joined a new school or simply grew up, observed, analysed and learned. Some of us didn't even recognise good when we found it because it was so alien to us, so we are still having to learn what it means.

Likewise, we often become so used to the addiction lifestyle that it starts to feel normal to us. Even those with more socially accepted addictions – such as nicotine or toxic foods – find that the addiction becomes normalised and ultimately takes control. It is eventually chosen over loved ones, career and even self. But we were designed for good, which means we can never be at peace in evil. Our brains, bodies and souls can't work properly in the wrong atmosphere.

Was good or evil most normal in your childhood context and experience? How has that affected you as an adult?

....

....

....

Think of a time when you were surrounded by evil, then think of a time when there was good around you. What do you notice about the way your brain, body and soul worked in those conditions?

....

....

....

>> >> >>

God gave Adam and Eve authority over the earth. They were to subdue, govern and reign over it. They were given the power to do this by God, and with power comes choice. Adam and Eve weren't God's prisoners; they had a way out if they wanted it. Even paradise can become a prison if you have no choice but to stay there. God desires mutual relationship, not forced fellowship. So he gave them the Tree of Life, from which they could eat and live in paradise forever, and the Tree of Knowledge of Good and Evil, from which they could choose a different way.[9] There are many Tree of Life opportunities in our lives that allow us to choose God (the oasis). But there are also many opportunities to choose the Tree of Knowledge of Good and Evil (the salt pan).

What have you chosen in your life that was like choosing the Tree of Knowledge of Good and Evil (or the salt pan)?

....

....

....

In what ways have you chosen – or are you now choosing – the Tree of Life (or the oasis)?

....

....

....

> > >

Knowledge Is Power

Adam and Eve chose to eat from the Tree of Knowledge of Good and Evil. Knowledge is power, right? The sad irony is that they already had power, but Satan manipulated them into craving a power that was equal to God's. He said, 'You will be just like God if you eat the fruit.' Instead of enjoying the power they had to reign over the animals and vegetation together, they went after greater power. They wanted to be equal with God, to reign over themselves and each other. As a result, they lost the power they already had, and instead of becoming their own masters they became slaves to sin and death.

Humanity has been fighting over scraps of power ever since; fighting to have power over itself and others. People continue to exhibit the same power struggles, even fighting over who had more power between Adam and Eve, like the squabble between siblings where the eldest says he is so perfect that the parents wanted more kids and the youngest says that her older brother was just a prototype, and then they produced an improvement. All the while, the perfect father (God) is crying out for them to simply love him and each other.

The truth is, all power comes from God. He delegated some of this power to Adam and Eve so they could reign over the earth together, but they surrendered that power to God's enemy, Satan the illusionist. Now all the earth is enslaved to the law of sin and death, and is completely powerless without God.[10]

When Adam and Eve ate, they chose to know evil. And since they had been given power and authority over the world, their choice affected the whole earth. They chose evil for themselves and for the world. They gave themselves and the whole earth into Satan's hands to become slaves. By choosing to know evil, they chose to serve the prince of evil. They used their God-given power to submit to God's enemy, handing him their power. This is why Satan has power over us but not over God.[11] We gave Satan our power, but no one has ever given him God's power. So in our own strength we are weak against Satan, but in God's strength Satan is no match for us. In our addiction we are powerless, but when we know the truth we are free because the truth is God's territory (we'll come back to this later).

Describe how it feels to be powerless against addiction once it has taken control of you.

....

....

....

Have you ever felt powerless against other forms of evil? Evil you've chosen or evil used against you? What forms were / are they?

....

....

....

>>>

The Oasis Versus the Salt Pan

God banished Adam and Eve from the Garden of Eden and had it guarded so they couldn't re-enter. This was most likely because the Tree of Life was still in the garden, and if they'd continued to eat its fruit they would have lived forever in a painful, corrupted version of what he had made for them. God was saving them from themselves, and from suffering the consequences of their actions for eternity.[12]

Nevertheless, he had a plan to lead humanity to a new, uncorrupted paradise. It would take a few millennia of earthly time, but his plan would help Adam and Eve, and their descendants, see evil for what it truly was, and to see their need for an *ezer* rescuer above them. At that point he would send Jesus to be the ultimate rescuer. The climax of God's rescue plan was to create the perfect sanctuary from evil within our hearts, making a way for us to one day be with him in paradise beyond this corrupted earth. On earth his rescue is the oasis in the desert, but one day his rescue will see the desert exchanged for a new and better paradise.

Now that we are separated from God, we yearn for the oasis of union with him; the joy unspeakable; the euphoria of his presence; the peace of being where we belong, in the place we were made to be. God's eternal design is within us, in our hearts. That's why we yearn for home; an eternity with him.[13] We instinctively long for more than what is in and around us, and so we should, because that yearning is supposed to drive us to seek God. But often along the way we find an alternative option.

The salt pan can take on many forms. It might be an anaesthetic for the longing soul, a distraction or ten, a way of rationalising away the longing, a disillusionment that leads us to dismiss expectation, or a trauma-induced hardness that is afraid to hope. Whatever form our salt pan takes, it always draws us away from the oasis of life.

But why did God's plan have to span thousands of years? Why didn't he just present a solution straight away? Because the effects of enslavement to evil meant that humanity wouldn't have understood the solution straight away. You see, when Adam and Eve chose evil, they chose corruption, confusion, pride, shame, fear, distortion, a cycle of addiction to further evil, and spiritual obliviousness. It would be like telling a blindfolded person planted in a stranger's house that they needed to find something they'd never heard of in a room they'd never been in. The blindfolded person wouldn't even know which room they were in to start with, let alone how to get to the room they needed to be in. And even if they found the right room, they wouldn't know that it was the right room or how to find what they were looking for.

The knowledge of good and evil made Adam and Eve blind in a place they didn't know, needing something they didn't understand. Knowledge of good and evil left *us* blind, in a place *we* don't know, needing something *we* don't understand . . . or at least didn't understand before we learned about God's plan. And led by the knowledge of good and evil, humanity doesn't even want God's solution.[14] That's why we need God to direct and describe; to place our hands on objects, walls and handles so we can feel them; to lead us into rooms so we can explore them; to help us experience the search so we know what we're looking for. But first he had to remove humanity from what had once been flawless paradise in order to save us from suffering the consequence of sin for all eternity.

Can you think of any times in your life when it seemed like God was taking you away from something good when he might actually have been saving you from yourself? Give an example or two.

....

....

....

Can you think of anything God led you to feel, experience and understand during your blindness, or anything he is leading you to feel, experience and understand now?

....

....

....

》 》 》

For some time, God let the consequences of Adam and Eve's choice play out. He was always there – loving, but not controlling. God has loved every single human throughout history, but he hated the evil Adam and Eve chose, and the evil their descendants subsequently chose.[15]

Have you ever loved a person but hated a bad choice they were making or something they were doing wrong? Did it hurt?

....

....

....

The more we love someone, the more we hate anything destructive they do or that is done to them, so imagine how much loving us, in our sinful world, must hurt God. What thoughts or feelings does that bring up for you?

....

....

....

Some years later, God prepared the next step in making a way back to a new paradise with him for anyone who wanted it. Enter Abraham. From the line of Abraham, God set apart a nation, the people of Israel, for three primary reasons:

1. As representatives of him, the one true God.
2. As a light in the darkness.
3. As proof that we need His divine *ezer* help and rescue.

A Representation of Himself

In order for the people of Israel to represent him, God demonstrated unconditional love, performed miracles, supernaturally provided shade, light and food, and disciplined them like a good parent, blessing and forgiving them no matter how often they rejected and dishonoured him. In order to reveal his nature, his ways and his kingdom to and through the Israelites, he gave them laws to demonstrate that he was not like the false gods commonly worshipped at that time. He revealed himself as a deity who accepted animal sacrifices but not child sacrifices, and who promoted community and equality, as opposed to division and abuse. While the godless norm was to furiously take a person's life if their punch took your tooth, God basically said, 'No, no! Just take a tooth for a tooth.'[16]

When we read the Old Testament through the lens of our modern context, the Israelites' lifestyle seems brutal and unjust. But God was meeting them where they were at in order to lead them somewhere better. The alternative 'normal' was far more barbaric and much darker, as we'd expect, given that Adam and Eve had chosen evil all those years earlier.

Gregory A. Boyd explores the Old Testament in his book, *Cross Vision*, and argues that God was not violent, but that he was cooperating with a violent people. He tells the true story of a couple of missionaries who flew out to visit a small tribe and discovered that the people there commonly practiced female genital mutilation (FGM) on baby girls, and that many of the girls died as a result. The people did not trust the missionaries when they first arrived. The couple needed time to prove their trustworthiness before they could challenge any deeply ingrained behaviours. But in the meantime, little girls were being mutilated and sometimes killed.

The couple decided to help the people perform the terrible act more safely, flying in surgical instruments and sanitisers, and teaching them safer methods. The missionaries hated partaking in such an awful act, but they knew that it would save more lives in the long run if they were able to meet the tribespeople where they were at and guide them from there, building trust along the way, rather than rejecting and confronting a fundamental aspect of their lifestyle from the off. Within three years, the whole tribe had heard the gospel, connected with Jesus and completely quit practising FGM.

Boyd uses this story to illustrate God's approach to the Israelites. God chose to meet them where they were at, painfully and temporarily engaging with some of their brutal, unjust practices, and playing the long game to win their trust and gradually guide them towards a better way.[17]

As well as demonstrating great love through his interactions with Israel, God also revealed his holiness. We will come back to holiness in Milestone Eleven, but for now we'll just acknowledge that God is perfect in a powerful way.

God also used the place where his presence was revealed to demonstrate his holiness. The people built a physical structure (first an enormous tent and then a temple), and God decreed that the centre – the Most Holy Place – was where he would rest his presence most powerfully, and that it was to remain sacred. There was a strong, thick veil around the Most Holy Place that separated people from the core of his presence because he was so righteous that his holiness was dangerous to any unrighteous people who got too close.[18]

Have you ever heard stories or read passages from the Old Testament and thought that God sounded like a monster? What does it tell you about God that he takes a long-term approach for our benefit, even though it hurts him and can make him look bad to people who don't understand what he's doing?[19]

....

....

....

Have you ever been misrepresented or hurt as a result of taking a long-term approach to helping someone? Or has anyone aside from God ever done that for you? What comes to mind when you think about it?

....

....

....

A Light in the Darkness

The nation of Israel was also established by God to be a light in the darkness. Even though the Israelites got so much wrong and kept betraying God, he blessed them time and time again, and he taught them valuable lessons along the way. When they obeyed God, they demonstrated that a community could thrive without people buying and selling each other; without lying, cheating and scheming; without rejecting the poor and the stranger; without taking more than they gave; and without sacrificing their children to the gods of other nations.

All such gods were actually Satan in the form of idols. According to the Bible, we either choose Satan in one of his many forms, or we choose God. We either choose the salt pan or the oasis. Satan the illusionist uses various disguises and tactics to lead us into darkness, sometimes even by making the darkness seem like light at first.

Isn't that so evident in addiction? The addictive activity or substance seems to offer light but only leads to darkness, and then that darkness becomes normal, until the tiniest sliver of light seems brighter than it really is. Adam and Eve discovering evil was the first step to evil becoming normal. From that point, darkness became normal.

If someone stays in a dark room for a long time, their eyes will adjust. If they stay even longer, their eyes will become so accustomed to the darkness that the tiniest sliver of dim light will seem bright. Eventually, they will forget what real light is like. And those who dwell in darkness are far more likely to stumble and hurt themselves than those who stay in the light.[20] When the Israelites did as God commanded, they were like a light flooding into a dark room.

Have the eyes of your soul adjusted to darkness? In what ways can you see that this darkness has become normal in your life or within yourself?

....

....

....

Has anyone been like a light in your darkness? Who, and how?

....

....

....

Proof That We Need God

The people of Israel also provided proof that we all need him. Even though they had been given countless laws and seen many miracles, they still screwed up. And even with the best intentions, discipline and guidance, we all screw up!

Through the nation of Israel, God showed us that humanity is enslaved to sin, that we cannot set ourselves free from it, and that no rule, willpower, blessing, discipline, reward, consequence or good leadership will change that; not even over thousands of years, where one generation should have been able to learn from the mistakes of the previous generation. If I ever find myself wondering why it took so long for Jesus to come, I remember that even after 2,000 years of Israel living without Jesus as the solution, still some people remained unconvinced of humanity's need for him.

Remember the blindfolded person in the stranger's house who needed to find something without knowing what it was? Through the nation of Israel, God proved that we were blind so that we would let him lead us to the solution. But part of the evil Adam and Eve unleashed was human pride, and that pride can make us adamant we're not blind, despite any degree of proof to the contrary.

Humanism is an ideology built around the pursuit of goodness without God, and much New-Age philosophy is based on an attempt to achieve morality, self-development and transcendence through anything but God's solution: Jesus. Whether we like it or not, Israel demonstrated that the law of sin and death is far mightier than any rules or good intentions; than willpower or vision boards; than good company or good leadership. All these things have value, but they just don't cut it. Not without Jesus. Through Israel, God revealed that we need a saviour.[21]

Have you ever come up with a solution to a big problem in the life of someone you cared about, only to find that they were convinced they didn't even have a problem? How did it feel?

....

....

....

Have you ever been too proud to admit that you needed help? What happened?

....

....

....

>>>

The Coming Christ

It took thousands of years and a set-apart nation to help a blindfolded humanity accept the correct diagnosis (slavery to evil and death) so that we would accept the correct remedy (Jesus). But despite his long-term approach, God has been pointing to Jesus – the remedy, the solution, the coming Saviour who was chosen before the world began – all along.[22]

From the Garden of Eden onwards, God has been setting out his plan for Jesus' earthly life, death and resurrection. He regularly signposted the impending arrival of Jesus throughout the Old Testament, hinting that he would settle humanity's debt, stand in the dock on our behalf, and take the rightful death sentence of our sin on himself. Jesus did this to make a way for those who were able to recognise evil for what it was; to realise our inability to conquer it ourselves; and to yearn for paradise enough to humbly accept his sacrifice and leadership.

For example, God spoke to the serpent (Satan) in the Garden of Eden and described Jesus as the 'offspring' of the woman (Mary), revealing that Jesus would crush the snake's head (defeat Satan once and for all).[23] There are a few hundred other prophecies about Jesus throughout the Old Testament.[24] Some are like obscure brushstrokes on the canvas of God's story, which don't make much sense until they're seen as part of the whole picture, while others are so obvious it's quite amazing.

For example, Isaiah knew the following was to happen: 'For to us a child is born, to us a son is given, and the government will be on his shoulders. And he will be called Wonderful Counsellor, Mighty God, Everlasting Father, Prince of Peace' and Micah prophesied that he'd be born in Bethlehem.[25] At the time of all these prophecies, most of God's people were able to put the pieces together, so they knew someone special was coming – a 'Messiah', a rescuer – but that was all. Some caught only a whiff of a hint, while others were completely oblivious, but many saw Jesus, by faith, before he was born on earth, and even looked to him for the salvation that hadn't yet come to fruition.

I'm usually quite good at finding my way on foot, but in the car I'm navigationally challenged. I use a satnav for most of my journeys and look at the road signs, yet somehow I often manage to miss the signposts, even though I'm specifically looking out for them! Other times I get so caught up singing along to my playlist at the top of my voice that I forget to keep an eye on the signs or satnav instructions.

On one occasion, my husband, Clyde, and I got lost and disagreed about how it had happened. We were equally convinced that a signpost we'd passed had said completely different things. As it happens, we were both wrong about what it had said. We had merely seen and remembered what we wanted to see and remember.

It can be much like that when it comes to God's signposts. We can be looking and still miss them, we can be too distracted to look, or we can be so stubborn about our own ideas about which way is right that we see what we want to see rather than what is actually in front of us.

Can you think of any times when God was trying to get your attention to reveal truth to you or help you, but you didn't see it? Maybe you're just starting to see it now. What events, people or 'coincidences' can you remember that might have been God's signposts?

....

....

....

Fulfilling Our Vows

Once God had – through Israel – revealed a correct diagnosis of the disease of evil, and slavery to the law of sin and death, and had helped humanity accept this diagnosis and its inability to heal singlehandedly, his next step was to reveal the remedy, the solution, the rescue plan, the Saviour: Jesus!

We have finally arrived at the New Testament. You'll see the Bible is split into two parts, two testaments. But what is a 'testament'? The word has two meanings. One relates to someone's story and what they witnessed. This is where we get the word 'testimony' from. The other meaning relates to a covenant, like a vow. Like a cheating spouse, the Israelites had well and truly broken their covenant with God as a result of their ongoing sin (God likens the nation of Israel to an unfaithful spouse in the Old Testament book of Hosea).

But once again, God was not caught off guard. He had always known they would break their vow to follow his ways because humanity is incapable of faithfulness to God while living under the law of sin and death. However, he also knew that we needed to see this for ourselves. Therefore, Jesus came as the second covenant – a new vow – in which he did the miraculous work required to fulfil the old covenant on our behalf.[26] He crushed sin once and for all, so we are now free to offer reciprocal vows of love and commitment to him if we so choose.

Have you ever tried really hard to stick to a commitment or promise and not been able to understand why you couldn't do it? From diets to wedding vows, from work projects to promises you made to your kids, list everything you have been unable to stick to.

....

....

....

What thoughts and feelings come up when you consider the idea that Jesus not only offers us a second chance but also gives us the ability to succeed; not only at recovery, but at commitment and at life in general?

....

....

....

Jesus was born on earth, exactly as God had prophesied in the Old Testament. Even so, he didn't come in the way people expected. The Israelites were expecting a warrior king with earthly wealth, power and status. Instead, he appeared with spiritual wealth, power and identity. But from an earthly perspective he appeared poor, vulnerable and meek.

Once again, God used his unique style to tell us something. The way Jesus was born told us that earthly wealth, power and status were redundant in the presence of spiritual wealth, power and identity. Jesus' success was all the more miraculous because he had no earthly benefits. Throughout history, people have bought fame with money, used power and status to coerce people, and used wealth and status to win favour, but Jesus used none of those earthly benefits. No one can point to anything to explain Jesus' success, except Jesus himself as God and man – spiritually wealthy, spiritually powerful and with a spiritual identity.

By coming as a helpless baby within an environment of poverty and chaos, Jesus was deliberately connecting with our lowness. He cut no corners and took no liberties in becoming like us. He showed us that he connects with every human; not only those with whom it would be advantageous or popular to establish a rapport.[27]

Have you ever felt you were at a disadvantage because you didn't have worldly wealth, power or status? What difference do you think spiritual wealth, power and identity would make in your life?

....

....

....

Have you ever felt too low to be lifted high? What thoughts and feelings arise as you ponder the idea that Jesus came the way he did to connect with those who have been brought low?

....

....

....

....

❯❯❯

All God, All Man

Hold up . . . Did I just say that Jesus is both God *and* man? Yup, indeed I did. And it's not even as if he's half and half, like some demigod or Marvel character – which is about as close to reality as fiction has come. The reality is far more supernatural. Jesus is 100 per cent God and 100 per cent human.

Check out the way this poem from Philippians 2:5-8 (in the Bible) puts it:

. . . Christ Jesus:

Who, being in very nature God,
    did not consider equality with God something to be
    used to his own advantage;
rather, he made himself nothing
    by taking the very nature of a servant,
    being made in human likeness.
And being found in appearance as a man,
    he humbled himself
    by becoming obedient to death—
        even death on a cross!

Completely God and completely human? God has a habit of simultaneously being two things that we see as oppositional. He's all-powerful, yet he has given us the power to make our own choices. He knows every detail of the future, yet our actions are not predetermined. He is completely gracious (blessing us even when we don't deserve it) and merciful (withholding the punishment we do deserve), yet he's also completely just. How can that be? How can someone be just if they offer undeserved blessing and withhold deserved punishment? The answer is Jesus, and the Bible explains how he achieves this, but it's super genius of God and it takes some searching to grasp it.

All of this – and much more – is incomprehensible from an earthly perspective, but utterly believable from a supernatural perspective. How can a fish comprehend cars or coffee? How can a baby comprehend continents or compensation? If we assume that all we know is all there is to know, we will comprehend very little of reality. Christian slogans and Bible verses such as 'God works in mysterious

50

ways' and 'his ways are higher than our ways' have been used in a lazy way by some to shut down or pacify valid questions, but we don't want to throw the baby out with the bath water. God's superiority and our humble limitations are difficult but powerful realities to grasp.

Jesus came to earth by the same means as his created people – out of one another and through the breath of God, the Holy Spirit. The difference is that Jesus is the fullness of humanity and the fullness of God. He couldn't have stood in our place and mediated with God on our behalf if he hadn't been one of us. Jesus' death and resurrection could not have turned every dynamic in heaven and earth on its head had he just been a man. It was through his humanity that he was able to represent us all, and through his divinity that he had the authority to take our sin on himself and graft his righteousness onto us.

Satan had a legal right to humanity because Adam and Eve handed it to him through the power of choice God had given them. To legally win us back, Jesus had to live a sinless life on earth. He couldn't have done this fairly if he had been anything less than fully human. And if he had been anything less than God, he wouldn't have been able to buy us back at such a high price: his blood. Only the blood of God is that weighty![28]

What stands out to you most about the poem we read from Philippians 2?

....

....

....

In what ways have you forgotten that there is more to life that what you personally know – like a fish that has no concept of anything beyond the ocean?

....

....

....

The New Testament tells us about the earthly life and ministry of Jesus through four different accounts. From birth to crucifixion, his life spanned thirty-three years, and in the three or so years that preceded his death he performed many miracles of physical, spiritual and psychological healing. He taught about the kingdom of God (his nature, ways and rule), and revealed himself as the radiance of God's glory and as an exact representation of God.[29] Jesus came as God with skin on; God approachable; God experienced at a human level. This means that whatever Jesus did, however he behaved, every choice he made and every word he spoke, was an expression of who God is.

Jesus taught through action, example, relationship and words. In all these ways he took the instruction of the Old Testament to another level – beyond the law into righteousness; beyond action, into the heart. As discussed earlier, the norm in Old Testament times was to take a *life* for a tooth, but God had told the people to take a *tooth* for a tooth. Having allowed more than 2,000 years for that to sink in, Jesus told the people to turn the other cheek.[30]

We Don't Deserve It

Although the Jewish people had proved they couldn't be good and keep all of the laws, there were some who did meticulously keep them. However, they were still far from righteous. There was a group of powerful Jewish leaders who you could say obsessed over the law, but Jesus compared them with white-washed tombs (among other things) because they looked good on the outside by keeping the rules, but their hearts were rotten.[31] They were slaves to sin, just like anyone else who hadn't experienced salvation.

As well as taking humanity to the next level of revelation as God continued to play the long game – a bit like the missionary couple with the tribe – Jesus also reinforced the reality that, without a divine rescue from the law of sin and death, humans could never escape their slavery to evil. Jesus explained that no one could enter the kingdom of God (be with him in paradise) unless they were truly righteous in heart and desire. But seeing as no one is righteous, how can we enter his kingdom? Through the divine exchange his death and resurrection made possible, which enabled him to pay for our sin in exchange for his own righteousness.[32]

Have you ever considered yourself good because you keep the rules, even though you have bad thoughts and desires? If so, how do you match up to Jesus' standard? Spend one whole day loving all your enemies, turning your cheek whenever someone hurts or offends you, feeling zero lust, revenge or toxic anger, being completely dependable and trustworthy, keeping every vow, loving others and yourself, loving God will all your heart, mind, soul and strength, and then come back to this question and record your experience.

....

....

....

....

....

Have you ever felt like you're too bad to have any chance at forgiveness from God? What thoughts and feelings arise from the idea that your identity can be in who Jesus is and not in who you are or what you do?

....

....

....

According to author Max Lucado, Jesus' death fulfilled at least fifteen prophecies.[33] It wasn't just a monumental moment on earth; it also went far beyond our small planet. So much has been written about Jesus' death there isn't a library that could contain it all. The way God does things sends us a message, and there are loads of messages from God in terms of the way Jesus died. This isn't the place to go into detail (even though the details are so awesome), but *He Chose the Nails* explores these messages of the cross beautifully, and there is also a list of recommended videos at the end of this milestone to explain Jesus' death in more detail.

For now, it's enough to know that his death was a supernatural event. The earth shook, thunder roared, tombs broke open and darkness fell during the daytime.[34] Another important thing happened as a symbol of the miracle Jesus was silently performing: the veil tore in two. Do you remember the thick veil I mentioned from the Old Testament? The one that kept impure people from being destroyed by God's perfection? Adam and Eve's decision to embrace evil created an invisible veil between us and God, and the veil in the physical temple God dwelt in was a visible symbol of this invisible phenomenon. So, just as the physical veil was torn when Jesus died, the invisible veil was also torn, making a way for us to enter God's presence. One day we will be with him in person, as Adam and Eve were, but in the meantime we are with him by his Holy Spirit, who lives within us when we choose Jesus. And the veil was torn top to bottom, which could be seen as a metaphor for how God at the highest point reaches down to us at the lowest.

Jesus didn't die for the deserving. That's the whole point – *no one* is deserving! That's what God's story shows us time and time again, all through the ages. We are so undeserving that we needed Jesus to die on our behalf to restore our relationship with God. He willingly laid down his life for the people who crucified him. People he had created. Maybe a good person would die to save a friend, but Jesus died for us while we were still enemies of God.[35]

Have you ever cursed, rejected or dismissed Jesus? What thoughts and feelings arise as you consider that Jesus was willing to die for you, knowing every single curse you would use against him, and every time you would reject and dismiss him?

....

....

....

Imagine Jesus looking into the eyes of those who were falsely accusing, betraying and hurting him, choosing to let it all happen for their good. What does that mean to you?

....

....

Alive Again

Three days later, Jesus rose from the dead! And yes, it was three days, although the celebration of Easter implies otherwise. Easter is not the literal anniversary of Jesus' death and resurrection (he did not die on a Friday and rise on a Sunday – the references to feasts and festivals tell us that). There were more than hundreds of witness accounts to corroborate the fact that he had risen.[36] As some of us are well aware, it only takes three witnesses in a criminal court to slam the door on someone and throw away the key. Jesus had more than 500!

You see, if Jesus wasn't resurrected, he wasn't really God, his plan didn't work and he was just an especially awesome human with special powers and powerful words. But those of us who have received the supernatural miracle of being 'born again' (which we're about to explore) know that the plan *did* work and the miracle *did* happen. The resurrection sealed the deal and cleared the debt that the cheque of his blood had paid for us. Moreover, God continues to resurrect people, purpose and relationships to this very day.

Have you experienced the miracle of spiritual rebirth? Have you been made righteous through receiving God's righteousness? If so, what was it like? If not, what do you see as the pros and cons of doing so?

....

....

....

....

What things or relationships would you love to see resurrected in you as a person or in your life?

....

....

....

>>>

After spending some quality time with the people closest to him, and reassuring them that they wouldn't be alone, Jesus left his earthly life to take up his seat at the right hand of God the Father.[37] Jesus is seated because his work is complete.[38] As he said on the cross, 'It is finished.'[39] A new way to connect with God had been created, a new solution to our sin was on offer and God's rescue plan was available to all. The veil had been torn in two. Now we have the Holy Spirit – the Spirit of Jesus, of God – with us on earth.

Why do you think Jesus left his earthly life and allowed his Holy Spirit to take his place? What benefits might there be to having the Holy Spirit instead of Jesus in physical form with us on earth?

....

....

....

....

Reconciliation With God

Jesus talked a lot about people following him, and in the early days after his resurrection his followers were known as people of 'the Way'.[40] This active and decisive following is central to the Christian life, but it is only possible if we agree to exchange our evil ways for his righteousness and enter a relationship with him. This comes about as a result of another thing Jesus talked about: being born again.

When we become born again, our previously dead human spirit is reborn and Jesus' Holy Spirit makes our hearts his home.[41] Everyone on earth has been born 'of water' (born in the natural, of a woman) or is going to be born that way within the next nine months. But not everyone on earth has been born 'of the Spirit', whereby the Holy Spirit supernaturally brings to life back to the human spirit that Adam and Eve's acceptance of evil had slain within us.[42]

So, what happens when we are born again? For one thing, we return to paradise. We have the promise of a return to an environmental paradise one day, further down the line in God's full plan. In the meantime, we can taste paradise internally, through our intimacy with the Holy Spirit. For another thing, the consequences of Jesus' work on the cross are broken down into what theology (the study of God) refers to as: substitution, forgiveness, propitiation, justification, atonement, reconciliation, adoption, redemption, restoration, regeneration, conviction, sanctification, glorification and salvation. A lot of those words may be new to you, but we've already covered some of them earlier in this book. Knowing the words (or being able to pronounce them) isn't what matters; it's what they mean that matters. So, let's just wrap it up.

Because Jesus became our substitute, dying instead of us, we are forgiven and justified (some people like to remember 'justified' as *just-as-if-I'd* never sinned').[43] As a result, God has made a way for us to be reconciled to him and to be one with him by his Spirit in us (atonement, or as some people say 'at-one-ment'). Those of us who have chosen to accept and follow Jesus have become children of God.

I've met a lot of people who have been adopted in the earthly sense, and I've witnessed very different effects of that in different situations. I know someone who was adopted by decent people who just didn't understand identity, so that child grew into an adult with a lot of confusion to work through. And I know someone who was so horrifically neglected before he was adopted that even though he is now one of the happiest people I've ever met, he still lives with the developmental challenges caused by that infant neglect. I also know a couple of people who were adopted into brilliant families but were haunted by a sense of conflict between their happy, healthy selves and their neglected, abandoned selves. And I know someone who was adopted out of terrible chaos, disfunction and abuse who had to work through a lot with his new parents but is now so calmly confident and humbly successful that people are shocked he ever experienced the childhood he did.

The latter case is the most similar to what happens when we are adopted by God. The effects of our former life don't instantly disappear, but our heavenly Father helps us work through them until we become better versions of ourselves. When we are adopted by God and filled with his Spirit, we become his children – making us heirs to his amazing kingdom, just like Jesus.[44]

Are you adopted? Or do you know someone who was? What do you think is the main difference between earthly adoption and spiritual adoption?

....

....

....

Redemption and Sanctification

In order for God to adopt us legally (righteously), Jesus had to redeem us. Adam and Eve effectively sold themselves to Satan the illusionist when they gave him their God-given power and chose to embrace evil, which left all of humanity destitute. But Jesus paid the highest possible price to buy us back by shedding his blood. This was a powerful act of redemption, of saving us.

Now that we are forgiven, saved, redeemed and adopted, the original human spirit is alive once again. However, we continue to battle with the 'flesh', or the 'carnal nature' – the part of us that is still seduced by darkness and distorted loves, or by trying to become god ourselves. Sanctification is the process of the human spirit winning the battle against sin. It is a process of spiritual formation, of growing stronger with the help of the Holy Spirit within us as the flesh or carnal nature gets weaker.

The result of this sanctification process is more fruit of the Spirit: love, joy, peace, forbearance, kindness, goodness, faithfulness, gentleness and self-control.[45] We will also be more resistant to 'lusts of the flesh', which are usually momentary forms of instant gratification with destructive effects, just like the substance or activity of your addiction. Sanctification makes us better people. It makes us more receptive in our relationship with God, as we inadvertently reject him less. This sanctification takes place through spiritual disciplines, such as prayer, worship and studying the Bible; through spiritual contemplation and action; through obedience to what our spiritual gut knows is right, even as our flesh rages in protest; and through our commitment to a spiritual community, with all the benefits it provides and all the sacrifices it requires.

There's an old illustration often used in counselling that asks: if two dogs of equal strength fight every day, how you determine which one will win? The answer is: the one you feed. Sanctification is similar, in that the choices we make feed either our spirit or our flesh. The difference for us is that sanctification is a work of the Holy Spirit. Our choices either cooperate with the Spirit's work, or hinder and reject it.[46]

In what ways would your life be different if you had more fruit of the Spirit and less lust of the flesh?

....

....

What have you been feeding the bad dog that you could stop this week?

....

....

....

Amazing Restoration

Amid all of this, a process of restoration is taking place. The restorative work of Jesus is not just for humanity but for the whole earth, because that's what Adam and Eve initially had authority over and invited destruction into. But on a personal level there is also a restoration of many things we have lost or damaged in this earthly life. God can restore purity, life and wholeness. Sometimes there is a restoration of specific things, such as relationships, dreams, abilities, positive feelings, health and even finances on occasion. But above all, it is a restoration of our relationship with God. Everything else flows out of that.

Jesus rightfully and legally won back the power that Adam and Eve surrendered to Satan, and will restore that power to whoever follows him and becomes one with him by his Spirit living within us. When Peter declares that Jesus is the Messiah in the New Testament, Jesus says that he will build his *ecclesia* (later interpreted as 'church') on the rock of Peter's revelation of who Jesus is.[47]

The word *ecclesia* originated a few hundred years before Jesus was born on earth, and was a political word used to describe an official democracy, through which the ruler at the time extended his decision-making power to the people, calling them out to assemble and reign together, with authority, under his authority.[48] In the same way, Jesus' church is a called-out people given authority and power under his authority and by his power. So even though Adam and Eve sold their power for an empty promise and ended up powerless against sin and death, Jesus has given our power back, as his *ecclesia* (church). We now have the power to choose God and all the good that comes with and from him.

Think of a time when you saw power being used for selfish gain or harm. Imagine if someone with the power to choose God had come into that situation and used that power well. What would have happened?

....

....

....

Maybe you've never thought of the Church the way I just described it. God never really wanted kings or temples; he wanted community. He wanted to be the sovereign God, the *ezer* rescuer and helper. He didn't want to be contained within an elaborate building like the ones other nations built for their false gods. But in the Old Testament, the Israelites really wanted a king and a temple.[49] That's why God met them where they were at – just as those missionaries we looked at earlier did with the tribespeople.

Jesus came to reassert God's desire for humans to be equal under his reign, and for God to be with us in an intimate way, rather than being contained in specific geographical locations. He made *us* his temple. Through the miraculous work of Jesus' incarnation (becoming human), death and resurrection, God made a way for us to become his dwelling place, by his Spirit. In some ways, we can now be even closer to God than Adam and Eve were before their knowledge of good and evil created the veil that divided humankind from God. God physically walked with Adam and Eve in the Garden of Eden, but he was outside of them. If we are born again, we have him *within* us. You can't get any closer than that!

Of course, in the 2,000 years since Jesus declared he would build his *ecclesia*, the Church has experienced its fair share of identity crises, the most prevailing of which is the fixation on geographical places and buildings. It is common to hear a building referred to as 'the house of God', but Jesus didn't merely move house – moving out of a temple or synagogue and into our church buildings. He made *people* his home. The Church of Christ has many functions, purposes, privileges and responsibilities, but more than anything it is God's house within his collective people. We are his body; his dwelling place.[50]

Have you ever met a Christian who truly lives as if he or she is a dwelling place of God, not just someone who 'goes to church'? What have you noticed about that person?

....

....

....

Finally, although we can experience internal paradise through God living in us during our time on earth, we will one day be in paradise – once we have left this earth and entered eternity. There we will live without the external context of a tainted, corrupted world, and our flesh will no longer threaten our own internal paradise or the paradisical environment for others. There will be no sin, war, abuse, betrayal, neglect, abandonment, abuse of power, corruption, manipulation, emptiness, angst or heartache. This will be a full restoration, known as 'glorification'. The Bible speaks of a new earth that his people will inhabit and reign over, where the Tree of Life is available.[51] It almost sounds like a Garden of Eden do-over, only it'll be better because we will all be one with God.[52]

Which thoughts and feelings arise as you picture what this new earth will be like?

....

....

....

So . . . that's the God story in a nutshell. Albeit quite a large nutshell!

In John 14:6, we read: 'Jesus answered, "I am the way and the truth and the life. No one comes to the Father except through me.' Jesus *is* the truth. By knowing the story of God and humanity, by understanding God's solution (Jesus) and choosing him, we partner with truth and can legally escape our bondage to Satan the illusionist. Jesus' act of redemption (buying us back from captivity) gives us a legal precedent to cut our union with Satan forever, like divorcing someone who has tricked us into marriage. A marriage in which we were sold as a commodity to an illusionist, with no legal rights. Jesus has given us the right to end our slavery by divorcing him and becoming children of God instead.[53]

If you have decided not to accept the gospel and give your life to Jesus, that by no means excludes you from the rest of this recovery journey. You can skip the prayers, appreciate the scriptures as ancient texts full of helpful wisdom and just let everything I have said ruminate as you continue to seek freedom from your addiction. I believe that God gave me this understanding, so I will repeatedly credit it to him, but when Jesus was on earth he healed many people who never followed him afterwards. This tells me that God wants you to have this gift of freedom, even if it doesn't ultimately lead you to him (though I believe that the fullness of eternal freedom is only possible through Christ). Just as anyone would fall if they walked off the edge of a cliff – regardless of whether or not they believed in gravity or the God who created it – so anyone can find freedom from addiction through the truth being unravelled in this course.

If you'd like to learn more or see some creative expressions of the Gospel, check out these QR codes:

Propaganda, G.O.S.P.E.L.:
https://youtu.be/jyYFxp7apl4

Alpha, Episode 3, Why Did Jesus Die:
https://www.youtube.com/watch?v=lIHqYqljKVw

The Bible Project, The Gospel:
https://www.youtube.com/watch?v=xrzq_X1NNaA

Billy Graham, The Cross:
https://www.youtube.com/watch?v=lMZLPa-wCIA

But What's Happened to Satan?

At the end of God's story, Satan is defeated, but he's like a criminal on death row, desperate to take down as much and as many as he can on the way to his final end. Satan cannot approach us all individually and personally, as he did with

Adam and Eve, because he is not omnipresent (everywhere at the same time, like God's presence). Neither is he all-knowing or all-powerful, as God is. So he conspires to use the world and our sinful nature to steal, kill and destroy.[54] Satan, the world, and our own sinful natures are the three battles we face. Christian leader and author John Mark Comer refers to these three battles as 'lies', or 'liars'.[55] It is only knowing the truth that can set us free from these lies.[56]

Satan uses a domino effect to tempt, accuse and deceive.[57] He takes what he knows about our sinful nature and triggers something in the world that becomes a system or an assumption that deceives and distracts us. He initiates false beliefs, social movements, cultural norms, desensitisations and dysfunctional coping mechanisms, all of which have a domino effect. They reduce the amount of warning people are given about the water in the salt pan and increase the availability of that salt water, all the while normalising the slow death it causes.

Never Enough

Throughout our lives, our environmental context perpetually pushes us towards addiction. People get rich by selling us things, but we won't buy them unless we think we're incomplete without them. The advertising starts with the media but gets carried by each of us until it is repeated in workplaces and school playgrounds. Eventually, it becomes normalised in every social place, and it constantly tells us one thing: we are not enough. We are not happy enough, good enough, attractive enough or strong enough. It tells us that others are more 'enough' than we are because they have what we don't, so if we have the same things we will also be enough. But no matter what we have, it is never enough.

The truth is, we all have an emptiness, an angst, a yearning for something beyond ourselves. But this is a God-given awareness, designed to lead us to him (the oasis) as the only way of being and having enough. When we follow the voices that tell us to try other ways of solving the ache, we make the people who sell them more money but our angst increases as we get further and further from God, who we were made to be completed by. The more we drink from the salt pan, the thirstier we get. Then we use the other things more and more, growing emptier and emptier, thirstier and thirstier. Before we know it the brain is damaged and we're addicted.

The salt pan ranges from socially acceptable overeating or popularity to hidden self-harm and purging; from legal drugs such as nicotine, pain medication and alcohol to illegal heroin, crack and meth. And then there's sex, gaming, shopping, work and various types of pill, powder, rock, inhalant and liquid. Whatever we are addicted to, it's ultimately the same cruel trick that is being played on us all. On the surface, from a human perspective, it's all about money and gaining power. But on a spiritual level it is initiated by Satan himself to kill, steal from and destroy us.

Something deep inside us still yearns for the oasis, but our sinful nature wants a quick, cheap, easy escape more than a long-term solution. The salt pan offers a brief moment of intense pleasure similar to the feeling God has been offering all along. With God the process leads to ongoing pleasure, but with drugs we move backwards from that short moment of pleasure into long-term misery.

We tell ourselves that maybe the oasis is just a mirage, too good to be true. We tell ourselves that the oasis is more of the same salt water, a similar type of deception. Perhaps he is just another crutch in a different form, no better than what is already right in front of us. Or we tell ourselves that someone will surely find and rescue us before it gets too bad. We reason that if the oasis is real and good it will come to us, instead of us having to go to it.

Until we stop.
Learn the truth.
And choose Jesus.

It is only then that we begin the process of transformation.

Dear God . . .

Thank you for giving humanity chance after chance. For giving *me* chance after chance.

Thank you for opening my eyes and sending me the perfect solution through your sacrifice. Thank you for making a way for me to be saved and free – for buying me back from slavery to sin and death – even at such an incredible price!

Open my spiritual eyes and ears to understand your gospel more deeply each day. I pray that what I have learned will become more than mental information; that it will become heart revelation.

Amen

You've achieved Milestone Six!

Statement of truth:

I recognise that an enemy provides false relief, but God sacrificed himself to provide true freedom.

'The thief comes only to steal and kill and destroy; I have come that they may have life, and have it to the full.'

John 10:10

Milestone Seven:

Embracing the Recovery Process

'The thief comes only to steal and kill and destroy; I have come that they may have life, and have it to the full.'

John 10:10

Process

When you piece together different parts of the New Testament (the last third of the Bible, starting with the book of Matthew when Jesus comes to earth), there is a strong theme that runs through it about our salvation. It's an ongoing process. We see that once we become followers of Jesus and are supernaturally 'born again'. We *have been* saved, we *are being* saved and we *will be* saved.

At the point of salvation, the human spirit comes back to life – or reawakens – and is saved. We are God-connected, corruption-free and heaven-bound. But the human soul – our mind, will and emotions – is still in the process of being saved, so that it can align with this fully saved human spirit through ongoing surrender and breakthrough. You see, God desires to lead us but not to dictate; to rule but not to control. So even after we have chosen him as the rightful king of our lives, we still have a hundred choices each day that either take us towards or away from that choice. God guides, equips and convicts us by his Spirit, moving us towards truth, justice and righteousness. But he will not force us to pursue these things.

Then one day in the future, on the other side of eternity, we will be saved from the darkness, corruption and consequences of a world under the influence of Satan the illusionist, and under the law of sin and death.

I've heard these latter two stages compared with D-Day and VE Day. Many historians have observed that World War

II was essentially won on D Day (6 June 1944), when the allied invasion of Normandy landed a fatal blow against the Nazi enemy, yet it wasn't until almost a year later (8 May 1945) that the soldiers were able to stop fighting because Hitler kept fighting until the bitter end. This reminds me of a scene from one of *The Lord of the Rings* films, where the defeated beast, the Balrog, plummets to its death but uses its tentacles to cause further destruction as it falls. Likewise, Christ has won the war against the enemy, yet Satan will do as much damage as he can before his ultimate demise. We are like the soldiers fighting on enemy lines, and we will continue to fight until the battle is really over and we are with God in paradise.

There is a process when it comes to salvation. There is a process to almost everything, in fact: from reproducing life to passing away; from healing a broken bone to ending a toxic relationship; from renovating a derelict house to starting a new career. In humans, in animals and in nature, there are countless processes! God's nature and ways are reflected in his creation. He is a God of process.

The same applies to addiction and addiction recovery. By pursuing recovery and working through all the parts of this course, you are embracing the process that will take you away from bondage and towards true freedom.

Process-zapping miracles do sometimes happen. For example, some people won't go through the reverse-craving graph from Milestone Three in Part One. They just suddenly find themselves free, with no desire at all for the substance or activity of their former addiction. In such cases, God has miraculously downloaded the truth, removed the illusion and healed the brain damage all at the same time. That's exactly what happened to my husband, and I'll share more about that in Milestone Eight. It is always exciting to see this happen, and I think most of us – if not *all* of us – would probably choose this over going through the process of recovery. But strength and growth are often found in the process, so while God can – and sometime does – miraculously circumvent the neurological and psychological process, he often guides and accompanies us through them instead.

Escaping the Chrysalis

My grandparents used to read a Christian devotional every morning or night. It was an A5 booklet with glossy paper, and each day of the year had its own message. I happened to read one of these pages one day, and it told a story I have never forgotten. It went something like this:

> A young boy noticed a chrysalis moving about and cracking, so he took a closer look. He could see that the butterfly inside was trying to break out of its temporary home but was struggling. He watched for a short while as the butterfly continued to struggle. He wanted to help, so he went and found a pair of tweezers. Then he bent down low, squinted and carefully used the tweezers to pry apart the cocoon and release the butterfly.
>
> Once the chrysalis had cracked open, the boy watched in awe as this beautiful butterfly spread its patterned wings and began to take flight. But as soon as the butterfly's wings flapped they stuck together, and the creature fell to the ground and died.
>
> If the boy had left the butterfly to continue its struggle, the time and effort of breaking open the chrysalis would have strengthened its wings for flight. You see, this struggle was an essential part of the process in the caterpillar's transformation from chrysalis to butterfly.

I experienced a time in my own life where God miraculously healed me from the deepest pit of depression in an instant. I could not have been more shocked and amazed if I'd seen a severed limb grow back, because I knew just how dark and real that depression had been. But there have also been times when God has led me through the process of healing from trauma with no sudden rescue.

When it came to addiction, there wasn't a sudden, process-cutting miracle for me. It was a constant struggle – a losing battle, over and over – until God started to show me the truths laid out in this True Freedom workbook. I begged God to take away my addictions. I had heard stories of him doing it for others and couldn't understand why he wouldn't do it for me, but I'm so grateful now. Because if he had just taken it away, he wouldn't have taught me what I learned. I would never have been able to pass that knowledge on to those in the residential programme Clyde and I run, and you wouldn't be reading this now as you journey towards your own true freedom. It was through my struggle that God created and strengthened the wings of this teaching.

Have you ever experienced a miracle? What happened?

....

....

....

....

....

What do you find hardest about the idea or reality of process?

....

....

....

In what areas of your life do you need this ongoing process of being saved?

....

....

....

Sometimes people are so sure that they have been saved that they neglect the ongoing process that comes after that initial decision. Others are so focused on the ongoing process of being saved that they forget they have already been saved. Some rush the process of growth, while others try to avoid it altogether.

Hardy Over High-Maintenance

We had lovely, sunny weather during the lockdown periods in 2020, and as I was saving lots of fuel money because we couldn't go out in the car, I decided to turn the ugly concrete square of our back garden into a pleasant space filled with life and colour. Clyde and I enthusiastically bought plants and flowers without waiting to find out what they were or how suitable they would be for potting in our space.

I called my green-fingered mum for advice on how to plant them and help them grow. She gave me some great general rules for irrigation and root strength, but there were also specific pointers for specific plants relating to soil type, sun exposure and so on. While we were discussing foliage, she said, 'Some plants are so hardy you can put them almost anywhere, in almost any way, and they'll grow, while others just need a little consideration to grow well. The plants you really want to avoid are the high-maintenance ones, which require such perfect conditions they rarely grow at all.'

Slow Growth Over Fast Growth

Many years ago, I was watching a television series about supermarket food, and in one episode tomatoes from four leading supermarkets were tested and compared with tomatoes grown on allotments. Now, you only have to sniff the air in a domestic greenhouse or when walking past a greengrocer to know that there's a big difference, but they were testing more than just taste and smell. The results showed that the supermarket tomatoes contained just a third of the nutrients. Why? Because, through the manipulation of environment and chemicals, they had been forced to grow unnaturally quickly to meet demand.

Supermarket Tomatoes Versus Poinsettias

Some of us are like high-maintenance plants, such as the poinsettia, which is perhaps partly sold as a Christmas plant because it's so difficult to keep and grow. Like the poinsettia, such people always find a reason not to grow. The soil wasn't right, the light wasn't perfect, the wind was too strong, the insects were too destructive. It's amazing how high-maintenance we can be when it comes to our personal growth. But when we behave like poinsettia people, demanding perfect conditions, we simply don't grow.

On the flip side, others are like supermarket tomatoes. They are in such a rush to grow, so determined to meet some internal or external demand, that they push and press everything into place and force growth more quickly than is natural. When we behave like supermarket tomato people, we may end up looking big and useful, but there will be a great emptiness and a profound lack of substance inside.

When it comes to personal growth, some people kick back and make no effort, while others push and strive to the point of exhaustion. Neither is God's way. His way for us to fulfil the process of being saved – of recovery – is to follow him. When he brings things up through the Bible, his Spirit, or through people and the circumstances around us, we shouldn't ignore them, but neither should we go hunting for things to confront without God's prompting.

The Old Testament proves that following God's law alone cannot save us. The New Testament is full of verses instructing us to grow, strengthen ourselves and mature, but every single one is to be read in light of the work Christ has done on our behalf. It should never be a lone pursuit that we either get arrogant about or kill ourselves trying to achieve. At the same time, God won't just do all the work for us. He won't take over or control us. We have to partner with him.

Supermarket tomato people try to rush ahead of God's natural process but just end up big and empty, while poinsettia people use any excuse to resist growth and end up small and withered. Although some people regularly behave like poinsettias or supermarket tomatoes, most of us are a combination of the two. For example, one person may try to force growth in terms of social maturity and how they behave with other people, while avoiding growth in the area of healing from trauma. Another may try to force inner healing, while avoiding dealing with a character flaw. Our focus needs to be on cooperation with God. It's important not to drag our heels, demanding perfect conditions, but it's also important not to rush the natural process, as if we were trying to get ahead of God.

Let's consider which way certain areas of your life are leaning right now. In which aspects of your life and recovery are you a poinsettia, demanding perfect conditions and blaming your environment when things don't go to plan? And in which aspects are you a supermarket tomato, impatiently driven by an internal or external demand to grow more quickly than is healthy?

Feel free to read the prayer below, then write down any aspects of your soul where you can see that you are forcing or resisting growth:

Dear God . . .

I pray that you would bring to my mind specific areas of my soul where I am trying to force growth. Please also show me the areas where I am trying to resist growth. Search me, oh God, and reveal what I need to see. Thank you for your Holy Spirit at work in me.

Amen

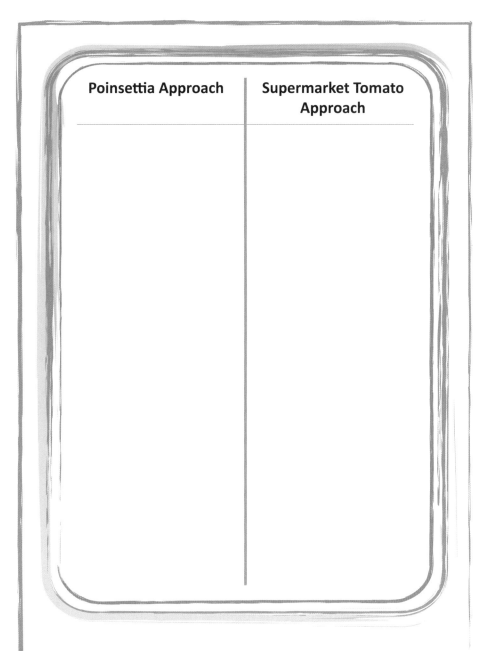

Poinsettia Approach	Supermarket Tomato Approach

The Temptation Scale

Do you remember the Temptation Scale from Milestone Four in Part One? Here it is again to jog your memory:

Temptation Scale

1. I really, *really* want it! It's taking everything I have to stop myself from using.

2. I want it, but I don't want the consequences.

3. I want it, but I love [insert anything you risk losing or causing harm to by using] too much.

4. I want it, but I don't *want* to want it any more.

5. I'm starting not to want it.

6. My feelings and thoughts are telling me I want it, but I understand that it's just my old brain pathways. If I remember that, I realise I don't actually want it at all.

7. I sometimes have the odd feeling or thought from the old pathways, but I know straightaway that I don't actually want it.

8. I don't really have any desire for it any more, but I'm aware of other things that could pull me back, such as [insert low self-worth, imposter syndrome, self-sabotage, unforgiveness, resentment, the effects of unresolved trauma, the name of a person or parent, or whatever it is that is still impacting you].

9. I want it so little that even calling it a temptation feels odd these days.

10. I'm not even slightly tempted by that substance or activity any more. In fact, I hate what it does to people. I'd rather eat my own vomit than fall for it again!

The Temptation Scale shows you what your growth is going to look like, spurs you on when it gets tough and reminds you that progress is a process. Be kind to yourself and celebrate how far you've already come.

Now, let's look at these points on the scale a little more closely.

1. **I really, *really* want it! It's taking everything I have to stop myself from using.**

You could say that every addict is at this first stage until he or she moves forward. Even if someone isn't yet seeking recovery, there's usually a reason not to use every so often – such as a child visitations, a court case, a funeral or simply determining to use the money for something else or attempting to remain in control – whether the addict succeeds in resisting or not.

But resisting this strong desire for the substance or activity of your addiction is the starting block for progress, because it is where every addict begins their recovery. The brain heals as the truth is known more and more, and the desire grows less and less. But short of a miracle, the first step is to do all you can to force yourself not to use any more. Anyone who gets through awful withdrawal symptoms while stuck at this stage of the Temptation Scale deserves a medal. Even activities or substances such as sugar, nicotine and gambling involve dopamine withdrawal, which is very real and physical, and is often made worse by not knowing what dopamine is (although we have actually seen countless people come off the likes of heroin easily with lots of prayer support). Resisting a substance or activity using willpower is unsustainable on its own, but is a necessary starting block on the journey to true freedom.

How does point one on the Temptation Scale make you feel?

....

....

If you've already passed this point, how does it feel to know you're already making good progress?

....

....

....

2. I want it, but I don't want the consequences.

You are still fully addicted, tricked and desperate for the substance or activity, but you can see what it has cost and continues to cost you – from family to health, from dignity to purpose. It is at this point in the process that people start saying things like, 'Addiction is giving up everything for one thing. Recovery is giving up one thing for everything.' But this type of reasoning won't be relevant to those who are progressing to true freedom by breaking the trick of addiction. Because you aren't giving anything up by leaving your addiction behind. You are only gaining. You are no longer under that illusion.

How does point two on the Temptation Scale make you feel?

....

....

If you've already passed this point, how does it feel to know you're already making good progress?

....

....

....

If you're not yet at this point, close your eyes, take some deep breaths, picture what it will be like and write down how that feels.

....

....

....

3. I want it, but I love [insert anything you risk losing or causing harm to by using] too much.

This point is similar to point two, but it revolves more specifically around deeper issues, such as other people being hurt by the addiction, a career or a physical ability. It goes beyond not wanting to live with the consequences of your addiction to actually choosing life. As I said in Part One, some people discourage addicts from entering recovery if they are doing it for anyone or anything but themselves, which makes sense if that person is prepared to remain an abstinent addict for the rest of their life. But if the addict is on the road to true freedom, it doesn't matter so much what started them on the road to recovery. Whatever the initial motive is, it is usually about choosing something over the substance or activity of the addiction. Therefore, the motive will always change once you know the truth because you'll never want that substance again, any more than you'd want to eat your vomit.

How does point three on the Temptation Scale make you feel?

....

....

If you've already passed this point, how does it feel to know you're already making good progress?

....

....

....

If you're not yet at this point, close your eyes, take some deep breaths, picture what it will be like and write down how that feels.

....

....

....

4. I want it, but I don't *want* to want it any more.

This is a real turning point on the Temptation Scale. The illusion of loving the substance or activity has started to crack, even though the compulsion for it is still strong. The brain's reward centre is still telling you to use or act –

screaming it throughout your mind, body and emotions – and the pathways in the brain are still directing you to do so at every turn, but your conscious awareness is starting to see it for what it really is: a con.

How does point four on the Temptation Scale make you feel?

....

....

If you've already passed this point, how does it feel to know you're already making good progress?

....

....

....

If you're not yet at this point, close your eyes, take some deep breaths, picture what it will be like and write down how that feels.

....

....

....

5. I'm starting not to want it.

This is an exciting point in anybody's True Freedom recovery journey, but it can also be a confusing and uncomfortable time due to the inner conflict you will inevitably feel. It can be a scary time, too, as the reality of life without the substance or activity starts to seem possible. There has been enough progress to start seeing life beyond your addiction, but there is still enough desire left to not yet truly see how great and free it will be. It's important to recognise this point as part of the process, allowing yourself to feel excited about the prospect of freedom but also knowing that true freedom won't feel like this because you haven't reached it yet. It will be better than you could possibly imagine, so keep going.

How does point five on the Temptation Scale make you feel?

....

....

If you've already passed this point, how does it feel to know you're already making good progress?

....

....

....

If you're not yet at this point, close your eyes, take some deep breaths, picture what it will be like and write down how that feels.

....

....

....

6. My feelings and thoughts are telling me I want it, but I understand that it's just my old brain pathways. If I remember that, I realise I don't actually want it at all.

You've started to understand the truth enough to gain some control over your addiction, but you're really having to *choose* to take control because the truth is still so new that it's not yet coming naturally. You have to keep reminding yourself, pretty strongly and frequently, but each time you do so it feels good. Try to see each thought and feeling of addiction as a chance to enjoy that feeling of gaining control over it.

How does point six on the Temptation Scale make you feel?

....

....

If you've already passed this point, how does it feel to know you're already making good progress?

....

....

....

If you're not yet at this point, close your eyes, take some deep breaths, picture what it will be like and write down how that feels.

....

....

....

7. **I sometimes have the odd feeling or thought from the old pathways, but I know straightaway that I don't actually want it**.

By this point you've really seen behind the curtain. You've learned how the trick works. You've got the upper hand! The truth has taken root as deeply as the lie had, and the lie has become so weak that you could almost swat it away like a pesky fly.

How does point seven on the Temptation Scale make you feel?

....

....

If you've already passed this point, how does it feel to know you're already making good progress?

....

....

....

If you're not yet at this point, close your eyes, take some deep breaths, picture what it will be like and write down how that feels.

....

....

....

8. **I don't really have any desire for it any more, but I'm aware of other things that could pull me back, such as [insert low self-worth, imposter syndrome, self-sabotage, unforgiveness, resentment, the effects of unresolved trauma, the name of a person or parent, or whatever it is that is still impacting you].**

This is a hugely important point to understand, as it's the reason behind many relapses. But for now, just know that addiction isn't an isolated issue. It's not a random disease that some people are born with. It's a trick that connects itself to many parts of our beings, usually with numerous triggers. It also connects itself to our identity, our pain, our relationships and our perceived worth. We cannot be completely free until we have fully disconnected it. This is one reason why people benefit from holistic Christian rehab even if they've been miraculously and instantly freed from addiction itself.

How does point eight on the Temptation Scale make you feel?

....

....

If you've already passed this point, how does it feel to know you're already making good progress?

....

....

....

If you're not yet at this point, close your eyes, take some deep breaths, picture what it will be like and write down how that feels.

....

....

....

9. I want it so little that even calling it a temptation feels odd these days.

This is an amazing point to have reached. Enjoy it! It feels so good to have power over an addiction. When you begin your recovery, still under the illusion it brings with it, you are powerless and it controls you. But as you learn the truth and fill your toolbox with tools of truth, you have power over your addiction. It's like that moment when the tables of power turn on a magician because a volunteer from the audience knows exactly how the trick works. But don't settle at this point. Issues from point eight can still pull you back from here, so you need to get to point ten to reach true freedom.

How does point nine on the Temptation Scale make you feel?

....

....

If you've already passed this point, how does it feel to know you're already making good progress?

....

....

....

If you're not yet at this point, close your eyes, take some deep breaths, picture what it will be like and write down how that feels.

....

....

....

10. **I'm not even slightly tempted by that substance or activity any more. In fact, I hate what it does to people. I'd rather eat my own vomit than fall for it again!**

This is the point of true freedom! Your whole world could fall out from beneath your feet and you would still never dream of using that substance or pursuing that activity again. You might do something else you regret – we're all human – but you'd never do *that*! In fact, an ex-addict at point ten is less likely to use the substance or activity of their former addiction than someone who has never been addicted in the first place because they see it for the trick that it is. They see that it has absolutely nothing to offer and only wants to rob from them and ruin their lives. If you've reached point ten, you would sooner eat dog faeces from the roadside than use that substance again. You are free!

How does point ten on the Temptation Scale make you feel?

....

....

If you're not yet at this point, close your eyes, take some deep breaths, picture what it will be like and write down how that feels.

....

....

....

Reaping What We Sow

There is one more thing we need to look at regarding process, which can be confusing during the process of addiction recovery, and also during the general recovery process from sin and pain. It's the issue of consequence, or reaping what we sow. We all instinctively know that actions have consequences, and that, regardless of reward and punishment, good and / or bad things can follow good and / or bad things. Some have made this consequence a religious concept and called it 'karma', others have made it entirely clinical and called it 'consequence', and others still have made it emotional, vengefully declaring that what goes around comes around, or that we get out what we put in.

The Bible acknowledges this action and consequence sequence as both natural and supernatural. In Galatians 6 (in the New Testament), farming is used as an illustration to state that we reap what we sow. This makes complete sense on a natural level. If I sow corn seeds, I cannot reap a harvest of beans. If I want beans, I need to sow bean seeds. And so it is in life. I'm not going to reap achievement if I sow quitting, and I'm not likely to reap loneliness if I sow kindness and connection with good company.

Another part of the New Testament, Romans 6, uses the illustration of a salary, but here the sense is more spiritual. The passage states that 'the wages of sin is death'. This means that our sinful efforts are rewarded with death. Doesn't that sound just like addiction? Many of us have heard comments along the lines of, 'If only you put as much effort into such and such as you put into scoring / gambling / secret eating.' Addiction becomes an effort, a work, and the salary is death on a spiritual level as well as on a physical level.

Galatians 6 (also in the New Testament) encourages us not to grow weary in doing good, for in due time we'll reap a harvest. But many of us grow weary during the recovery process because the harvest takes so long to grow. I've seen people give up because something bad 'came around' and made them doubt the good they were doing. A wonderful young woman I knew was working very hard at sowing good seed, but a wage slip of death turned up in the form of horrendous nightmares and internal pain. She couldn't understand how this bad thing was happening when she was sowing so much good. When I heard about this, I suddenly thought about online deliveries. Bear with me . . . this will make sense!

During periods of lockdown, most of us became more accustomed to ordering goods online and having items delivered to the door. But did you notice the way different deliveries arrived at different times, even if you ordered them on the same day? Sometimes I would order something well in advance and it would arrive the next day, but by the time something else was delivered I no longer needed it. Sometimes the consequences of our actions are the same. They don't all come at the same time, directly after the action. The results of our choices don't all come at the same point after we have made that choice. Don't give up on the good deliveries that seem to take longer than you expected, and don't feel discouraged when deliveries for your former bad choices get delayed and turn up just when things were starting to go well.

Sometimes it can take years to reap what we have sown. Some good consequences will appear more quickly than that, yet they rarely happen immediately. We order misery or goodness whenever we like, but the delivery sometimes takes a while. As a result, you may find yourself living in misery even though you're doing all the right things, because you're putting in an order for goodness that will be delivered in the future. Right now you're taking delivery of the misery you ordered before you started doing the right things.

Often people find themselves in the right place at the right time (such as a rehab centre or beginning a new life in some other way), but they're confused. They wonder if they've got it all wrong because they feel sad, anxious, overwhelmed, depressed, frustrated, bored, aggrieved and more. But those feelings may simply be the arrival of a former order, when a bad choice was made. How tragic it is when people give up on their current purchases and start ordering misery again because they don't immediately receive their good orders.

Well into his time in rehab, my husband Clyde received a parcel. He was excited, wondering what it might be. He opened it to find a pair of blood-soaked white jeans inside. After many months, the police had decided to return his property from a time when he had been attacked in relation to his drug-taking. He had been doing so well in rehab, sowing good seed and placing good orders, when an old, miserable consequence was delivered to his door. If he had taken that parcel as evidence of a bad harvest from all his good seed, he would have stopped sowing the good seed, and who knows where he'd be now . . . or even *who* he'd be. Thankfully, he realised that old consequences sometimes get delivered way after the order is placed, and he used the experience to praise God that the good consequences of his new life and choices would keep on coming long into his future. He went from reaping negativity, misery and pain to reaping positivity, joy and blessing, and then he went on to become positive, joyful and a blessing to others. He not only *reaped* what he had sown; he *became* it.

Many people spend a lot of their addicted lives sowing bad things, and not only do they reap those things, but they gradually become them. But if you keep sowing love, you won't just reap love; you will gradually become a loving person. If you keep sowing self-control, you won't just reap self-control; you will gradually become a self-controlled person.

However, there will always be delayed bad deliveries. Whether they come in the form of nightmares, bloody trousers or bad character traits you still have, the thing that really matters is what you're sowing now, and therefore what you're becoming. Which leads us neatly on to the next milestone.

Dear God . . .

Thank you for your patience through the process of my recovery. Please increase my own patience.

I ask that you would miraculously and suddenly perform healing works on my soul and brain if that is your will, but I thank you for the miracle of process and for your perfect wisdom if not.

Thank you for making the recovery process doubly worth it, because not only does it lead to goodness in the long run, but it can also produce goodness as it unfolds.

Please help me to learn and absorb the truths of this milestone so I can keep a good perspective through the highs and the lows of my recovery process.

Amen

You've achieved Milestone Seven!

Statement of truth:

I accept and appreciate the struggles and joys of process for all the good it can produce in me.

'The thief comes only to steal and kill and destroy; I have come that they may have life, and have it to the full.'

John 10:10

Milestone Eight:

Choosing to Be Truly Transformed

'The thief comes only to steal and kill and destroy; I have come that they may have life, and have it to the full.'

John 10:10

Transformation

Most of us want to change. We don't just want to be free from addiction; we want to be joyful, kind, strong, positive, admirable and fruitful. We want to leave places and people better than we found them. Even if we don't realise it, we want to be like Jesus. And then, when we meet Jesus or people who are like him, we want the same likeness even more.

When we decide to follow Jesus, we stop conforming to the world, which is great! Romans 12:2 in the Bible says: 'Do not conform to the pattern of this world, but be transformed by the renewing of your mind.' The problem comes when we start *conforming* to Christianity – or to the recovery process – instead of being *transformed*.

> **The world wants us to be conformed.**
> **God wants us to be transformed.**

What's the difference?

Well, let's look first at what it means to conform. Earlier in the book of Romans, the Bible uses the word 'conform' in a good way. Romans 8:29 says that we are conformed to the image of Christ. But Romans 12:2 tells us not to conform to the pattern of the world. Do you remember in Part One when we learned that the Bible was written in koine Greek – a language that often has several words where we only have one? Back then we were talking about the word 'knowledge' and how koine Greek had different words for different types of knowledge. Likewise, while we only have one word for 'conform', koine Greek has two. The difference is important because it could spell the difference between living in true freedom and just appearing to be free. It could spell the difference between being an ex-addict with tons of experience, empathy, gratitude and zero temptation to ever use again, or remaining an addict and forcing yourself not to use, then relapsing, forcing, relapsing and forcing.

The good type of conforming (Romans 8:29) means 'to morph into' (the Greek word is *summorphos*, which actually contains the word 'morph' and involves developing 'the same essential nature').[58] The other type of conforming (Romans 12:2) means 'to fashion oneself according to something' (the Greek word is *suschématizó*, which contains the word 'schema', which is to do with how we present ourselves).[59] So, to conform to the world is to dress and act like the world, but to conform to Christ's image is to become like Him. This is true transformation.

God's ways are not the world's ways. The world seeks to conform us so that we dress and act like everyone in it, but God seeks to transform us from the inside out. Freedom from addiction is no different. It comes not from fashioning ourselves in a different way by dressing and acting as if we were free, but from being transformed and *actually* becoming free.

Too often, new Christians – addicts or otherwise, all of whom are in recovery from sin and life's pain – enter God's kingdom feeling like they've got to act as though they're

Christians. They feel they have to pretend that they're healed and free, that they don't sin any more, and that they're full of the fruits of the Spirit, such as goodness, kindness and self-control. This is tragic, because acting like you're new can stop you actually becoming new.

How do we falsely conform?

We falsely conform by relying on willpower and by pretending to be fixed when we're not. Of course, there will always be times when we have to use willpower to do the right thing, even if it's not coming from a genuinely changed heart. For example, if you're extremely angry with your child, you may need to use willpower to stop yourself lashing out, or if you're incredibly nervous about an interview, you may need willpower to walk through the door and smile at your interviewers. There will be times when we have to act differently from what's really in our hearts.

Addiction recovery starts with saying no to what we really want. That's an essential step (except for in miraculous circumstances, or on occasions when people just suddenly realise the truth and are instantly set free). Sometimes willpower provides that temporary wall around the edge of the cliff that the hypnotised person kept walking off in Part One. It certainly has its usefulness at times. The problem arises when we act differently from who we really are, because that prevents God from actually transforming us. Many people in recovery quickly learn how to sound spiritual and appear strong, but by acting that way they inhibit God from dealing with the things that are buried deep within them.

Have you ever fashioned yourself to look like someone you're not or to look like the people around you? How did that feel?

....

....

....

My husband Clyde experienced a process-cutting miracle for his drug addiction. Having met Jesus in prison, he was set free from his addictions to heroin and crack without any withdrawal or craving. Years later, however, a different addiction he'd been battling from a young age threatened to destroy the life he loved.

He had managed to keep his complex sexual addiction under control since becoming a follower of Jesus by using willpower and behaviour modification, but he wasn't actually free of it. By conforming rather than transforming, he had prevented himself from going through the necessary process of healing and recovery. He was kidding himself that he had it all under control, when the whole time he was sinking deeper and deeper, just like the fly in the pitcher plant in Part One.

For years he tried to keep this secret, controlling it as best he could with willpower, and all the while hoping God would just take it away, as he had done with the heroin and crack addiction. But the longer he blocked out God's process, the more the addiction controlled him – conforming him, against his will, to *its* ways and twisting him into someone he didn't want to be. Until one day he confessed all and sought help. It was then that the healing process of recovery began. Clyde is now truly free from sexual addiction, so much so that he is probably the purest person in any room sexually, because God removed the deception and illusion of sexual brokenness that plagues most people to some degree.

What he and I learned through his recovery process was powerful and made us both stronger, as God's process always does. But it never would have happened if he hadn't kept trying to control it with willpower. Even though his heart was in the right place, his motives were good and he prayerfully sought God's help all along, he was unwittingly blocking God's assistance by merely conforming to what appeared to be right instead of admitting where he really was so that God could transform him over time. I've lost count of the number of times I've done the same thing; not just with addiction, but in many aspects of my life and character that weren't what I wanted them to be.

Habitual behaviour modification is impossible alongside genuine authenticity, as it always requires some degree of pretence. Transformation is not possible from a fake starting point. It takes vulnerable authenticity. Getting where you want to be starts with knowing where you are. And *accepting* where you are.

If I asked a friend for directions to a place I wanted to go but told him I was starting off somewhere different from where I really was, his directions would not get me where I wanted to go. God knows exactly where you really are, but he is truth, so he won't pretend along with you. He loves you too much to let you think he's ashamed of you the way that you are ashamed of yourself, or to let you stay in a place of darkness. God's starting point is to help you be honest about *your* starting point. That honesty represents the glorious start of your genuine transformation.

Have you ever made this mistake? Have you ever tried to get to your destination by pretending you were already there? What happened?

....

....

....

Renewing Our Minds

Sadly, Western governments help and encourage us to negatively conform when it comes to addiction, which stops us from being transformed. When we use methadone, nicotine replacement therapy (patches, gum, vapes), opiate blockers and so on, we are preventing transformation from taking place. Not only are we keeping the brain's reward system damaged and increasing the addictive pathways, but we are further convincing ourselves that the substance of our addiction is irresistible. We are using drugs to force ourselves not to use drugs, or to conform to an appearance of non-addiction without actually being free from addiction. This only makes sense for people who are still under the illusion, including non-addicts who are under the illusion that the substance or activity provides something irresistible to the person who 'needs' it.

When you do recovery God's way, you must be real with yourself and others about what your heart really wants, and open to God changing your heart – transforming you – over time. God doesn't want you to act like a Christian; he wants you to become like Christ. He doesn't want you to act like you're a new creation; he wants you to be transformed into the new creation he has made you.

God doesn't want you to live a life throughout which you merely resist the sin, substance or activity you really desire; he wants to open your eyes so you no longer desire it. You might be able to 'fake it till you make it' at a party or an interview, but that won't cut it in recovery or in any real kind of relationship, and it certainly won't help you as a disciple (follower) of Jesus.

What is the essence of your true self before God right now? What are your deepest desires, your hardest struggles, your strongest loves, your worst pains and your biggest dreams?

....

....

....

How can we be transformed? By the renewing of our minds.

As Romans 12:2 says: 'Do not conform to the pattern of this world, but be transformed by the renewing of your mind. Then you will be able to test and approve what God's will is – his good, pleasing and perfect will.'

The Root of the Problem

An eccentric, multibillionaire couple had two gardens. His was full of apple trees and hers was full of pear trees. One day they decided they wanted to grow apples in her pear garden and pears in his apple garden. They each hired a staff member: Ash to grow apples in the pear garden and Sam to grow pears in the apple garden.

On day one, the hired hands sat and walked around the garden they had been sent to work in, trying to figure out how to earn the money they had been offered. On day two, Ash turned up with a plan, feeling all fresh-faced and excited. Sam turned up with a big spade and a wheelbarrow. By the end of the day, both were exhausted and went to see what the other had achieved, but not much had changed.

After a week, they again went to see how the other was getting on. Ash couldn't believe how little Sam had done! He could see lots of evidence of digging, and there were exposed tree roots, but there were still apples everywhere! Ash sniggered, wondering if both wages might be up for grabs if the rich couple handed both gardens over to the most successful gardener. Meanwhile, Sam was equally shocked as she looked around the pear garden, where it was evident that Ash had merely plucked all the pears off the trees.

A few weeks later, Ash was at home relaxing. He felt satisfied that he had got rid of all the pears but was wondering how to make apples grow in their place. Sam had started digging up enough apple trees to allow her to turn the soil and start planting pear trees. Day after day she continued to dig up the old trees and plant new ones.

Ash eventually returned to the pear garden and was horrified at the sight of new pears growing on the trees after all the effort he had made to remove them. He wandered over to Sam's garden and realised what Sam had been doing all along. Months had passed by this point and Ash was in a rush to solve his problem without having to dig up any trees so late in the game. The couple would be coming back to investigate the gardens soon! So he carried on plucking pears, one after another, day after day. But the work was exhausting and he still wasn't really solving the problem. In desperation, Ash bought some red-and-white paint, mixed up various shades of pink, then proceeded to paint one pear after another in an attempt to make them look like rosy apples.

More months ticked by, and Sam finally managed to remove all the apple trees. Some of the newly planted pear tree shrubs were poking up out of the soil, but the garden still looked bare. It mostly looked like vast amounts of soil, with nothing to be proud of. However, she was full of hope and felt a sense of real achievement.

Meanwhile, Poor Ash spent most of his days picking pears off the trees, repainting them when the rain washed the colour off, or getting rid of the seeds as they ripened and dropped to the ground in order to prevent them from falling into the good soil and becoming new pear trees.

The couple returned to their gardens after a full year to see what progress had been made. They were absolutely thrilled to see new pear trees starting to grow in the former apple garden. But moving on to the pear garden, they were devastated! All they saw was an abundance of rotten fruit that had been left on the ground, blocking the potential for new pear trees in the soil underneath.

Both gardeners had worked hard, but Ash had tried to get rid of the unwanted fruit without removing the root of the problem. Then he had panicked and simply pretended to have made a change. Sam, on the other hand, hadn't had much to show for all her efforts during the early stages of the project, but amazing results had soon transpired. The couple paid Sam and handed her the pear garden to turn into an apple garden. Ash left empty-handed.

Toxic beliefs, patterns and perspectives have taken root within our true selves and keep producing negative behaviours. Using willpower in an attempt to change our behaviour is futile. It's like ripping pears off a pear tree because you want the tree to grow apples, but just ending up with more pears. Or like trying to paint your pears to look like apples, which results in a rotting mess.

The only way to stop producing the fruit (behaviour) you don't want is to dig up the root of the tree (removing the toxic belief completely). And the only way to grow the fruit you really want is to plant and nurture a new tree (a healthy belief). The more wrong trees removed and right trees planted and nurtured, the more transformed your garden will become.

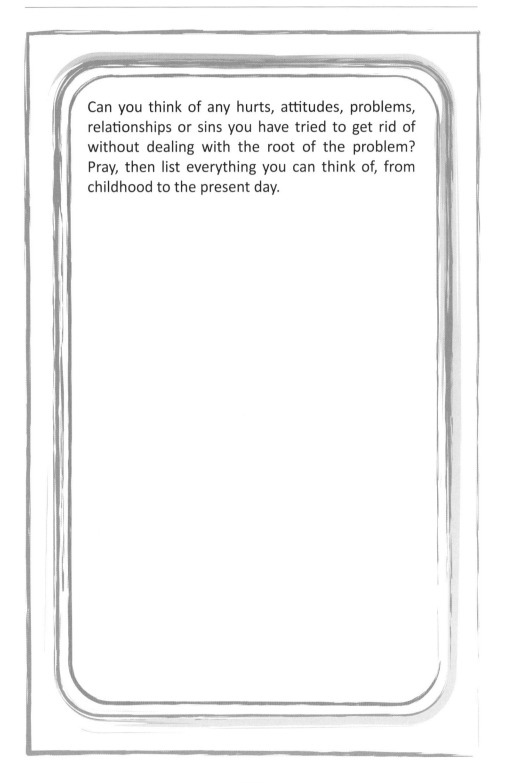

Can you think of any hurts, attitudes, problems, relationships or sins you have tried to get rid of without dealing with the root of the problem? Pray, then list everything you can think of, from childhood to the present day.

Can you think of any hurts, attitudes, problems, relationships or sins you have tried to cover up by pretending they were something else? Pray, then list everything you can think of, from childhood to the present day.

How did situations work out when you tried to get rid of the problem without dealing with the root, or when you tried to make it look like something it wasn't? Write down any words that come to mind.

If we want to renew our minds the Romans 12:2 way, we must dig up the old and plant the new. In reality, it's not just addicts who need renewed minds, because we are all affected by Satan, the world and our own sinful natures. Did you know that the average person has roughly 60,000 thoughts a day, eighty per cent of which are statistically negative and ninety per cent of which are repetitive?[60] Imagine the difference it would make if we were able to change just some of those to begin with and more over time.

What's really cool is that addicts have a big, urgent reason to take this stuff seriously, so they often end up with the skills and experience to rip up their bad trees and plant good ones in half the time, and with considerably less effort. Just like our muscles, the brain gets better at things with practice, as does the mind (I'll explain the difference between the brain and the mind in the next subsection). I've seen many addicts learn to renew their minds to such an extent that when their addiction is overcome their minds are so sharp and clean they can deal with much of the 'normal' bad thinking quite easily. Many non-addicts never learn to deal with those issues, which prevents them from becoming amazing friends, leaders, spouses, parents, workers and mentors.

How Do We Start Renewing Our Minds?

Communication pathologist and cognitive neuroscientist, Dr Caroline Leaf, explains that the possible rewiring of the brain discovered by neuroscientists lines up with the scriptural concept of renewing the mind.[61] The mind is responsible for the conscious thinking, analysing, imagining, processing, daydreaming, judging and reasoning we do, all of which takes place in the brain. So it starts with the mind and happens in the brain, but whatever is already in the brain influences the mind. I once heard someone say that asking where the soul is in the body is like asking where the music is in the organ. I guess the same could apply if someone asked where the mind can be found in the brain.

First we're going to investigate how renewal of the mind works in our conscious thinking (the mind), and then we'll investigate what that looks like in our unconscious thinking (the brain), because once we understand how both elements work we will become less vulnerable to discouragement and an overall sense of powerlessness.

We already know that what we believe is at the root of how we feel and behave, and renewing the mind has a lot to do with realigning our faulty beliefs. A book called *Truthformation*, written by my former local church leader (and mentor, along with his brilliant wife Dawn) is based on the premise that we are transformed by truth. John explains that the beginning of his ministry was frustrated by attempts to help people grow through various means without looking into the root beliefs that were driving them.[62] From what I've witnessed over a couple of decades of local church involvement, John's self-confessed early mistake is about as common as bread!

Strangely, even though I've long applied the correct approach when it comes to other people, I've made the same mistake many times when dealing with myself. Because this mistake is so common, and because transformation through knowing truth is so crucial, I'm going to borrow John's word, 'truthformation', from now on (with his permission).

Out With the Bad, In With the Good

But how do we renew our minds so they move away from the bad roots of misaligned beliefs and towards the good roots of truth? The process begins with a biblical practice that is difficult at first but becomes easier over time, until eventually it feels very natural. It's the practice of taking our thoughts captive to make them obedient to Christ, as the Bible implores us to do.[63]

But what does that actually mean? It means taking each questionable thought by the scruff of its neck, marching it into the courtroom of God and letting Jesus be the judge of whether it is true or not, or whether the root of the thought is true or not. Sometimes this happens as part of a process – through listening to God and others, reading the Bible, praying and receiving wise counsel – and sometimes it happens through an instantaneous decision to present that specific thought to Jesus and ask Him to judge it, listening out for the Holy Spirit's response and seeking a response through God's words in the Bible. Jesus then determines whether the thought is free to go on in truth or should be cast away as false.

Because Jesus is the King of kings – God with skin on – only he has the authority to correctly judge whether our thoughts are true or false. And because he is love – having proved the greatest love by dying for us while we were his enemies – we know that he is a trustworthy judge.

When we practise the biblical principle of capturing our thoughts and making them obedient to Christ, that's a conscious, intentional act of the mind, which leads to a subconscious rewiring of the brain. This amounts to truthformation: being transformed by the renewal of our minds.

I found it so powerful when I started to understand what was happening in my brain as I chose to take my thoughts captive and pursue the truth, even though I couldn't physically see it happening. No longer were recovery, growth and soul healing obscure aims that seemed slightly out of reach, no matter how closely I followed the process. When our brokenness is so ingrained, deep and normal to us, transformation can seem like a pipe dream, especially when we don't see it happening day after day or understand what is going on behind the scenes. But once I knew how it worked, I felt confident that change was gradually taking place because I could picture the brain activity by recalling images such as the scans in Part One and imagining what was happening in my brain according to scientific and biblical reality. Then later on I began to see it taking effect in my life.

Do you remember the mountain watercourse analogy I used in Part One? I said that a brain pathway is like a watercourse flowing down a mountain. The rainfall (a trigger) lands on top of the mountain and naturally courses along a route already carved out for it (a thought) until it runs down into a river (a reaction). How often do you do something, feel a certain way or come to a particular conclusion, only to wonder why? For example, maybe you flinch every time someone makes a sudden movement. If you grew up in a violent home or under threat of violence, there is probably a pathway in your brain that takes this rainfall (the sudden movement) and leads it down the watercourse (the pathway created by repeated experience and subsequent thought) into the river of reaction (fight or flight).

In addiction there are many watercourses that lead to the same river. More and more rainfall runs down into the same reaction. Almost everything becomes a trigger – from stress to boredom; from tragedy to celebration – and an increasing number of watercourses lead to the river of whatever substance or activity you are addicted to.

But as I mentioned in Part One, neuroplasticity is the scientific discovery of what God already knew: the fact that our pathways can change! We can close one watercourse down and open a new one.

The Toxic Thought Pathway

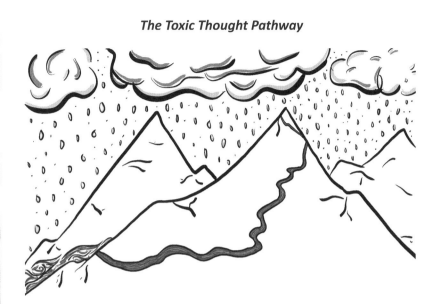

For the sake of simplicity, let's say that there is only one watercourse pathway leading the trigger rainfall to the river of addiction. The more water that goes down the path, the deeper the path gets and the more water goes down it, and so on. Sadly, a lot of addiction pathways attach themselves to old pathways that stem back to childhood.

For example, if from an early age you have believed the lie that you're not valuable, that will have become a strong, deep pathway and the lie of addiction can flow out of that. 'Since I'm so worthless anyway, I might as well . . .' This is one of the main reasons why addiction recovery is often about a much deeper form of recovery from whatever lies our bad experiences have taught us.

Creating a New Thought Pathway

If we want to challenge our deep-rooted, negative beliefs, we have to start creating a new channel, a new pathway, for the rainfall to run down. To do this we must first become conscious of the bad thoughts we're thinking, which the Holy Spirit will guide us in. Then we must take those thoughts captive and make them obedient to Christ, as described earlier. If he says it's based on a lie in some way (he will reveal this to us as we read the Bible, through his Spirit living within us or through other Christians, although what he says will always line up with the Bible), we must start to create a new pathway by thinking what is true instead of continuing to believe the bad thought, which is based on a lie. Over time, the old watercourse (brain pathway) becomes weaker because it's not being used as much and the new watercourse becomes stronger as more and more rainfall (triggers) flows down that new watercourse until a completely new river (reaction) is created.

Blocking the Old Pathway

Sometimes we need to do something proactive to catch the thought, feeling or unction and stop it in its tracks so we can redirect it. This is like dumping a huge rock on top of the watercourse we need to block. This makes it harder for the rainfall to follow the bad watercourse that leads to the wrong river.

For some people, literally shouting the word 'Stop!' works well, especially if they're in a residential recovery programme where everyone around them is on the same journey. For others it really helps to stick truth-filled Post-It notes around the places they spend the most time, so they are repeatedly reading the truth and deepening the new pathway. For most people it is good to have a mental image (such as the salt pan in the desert, a loved one walking off the cliff edge, or another image from this workbook that resonates); a specific scripture (such as Deuteronomy 30:19, John 10:10, James 1:15 or Galatians 5:17); or a sentence that wraps up the truth in a way that has a strong impact. It could be any sentence from this workbook or the personal statement of truth you created for yourself in Part One.

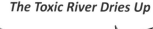

The Toxic River Dries Up

The end result is a dormant watercourse (toxic pathway) leading to a sparse river (toxic reaction), along with a thriving new watercourse (healthy pathway) leading to a plentiful new river (healthy reaction).

The Bible tells us to think about things that are true, noble, right, pure, lovely, admirable, excellent and praiseworthy.[64] Long before science discovered it, and even though the Bible's authors didn't realise it, God knew that the more we think about the things that fall within that list, the more healthy pathways and the less toxic pathways our brains will have. This means that we will heal, grow and react in better ways. How cool is it that the Bible's authors were writing instructions they didn't fully understand the power of? The God of all knowledge has given us principles in his word that we get to enjoy investigating, like a cosmic game of hide and seek. He gave us the keys before we even knew about the lock's mechanisms.

The Bible also tells us not to get tired of doing good because in time we will be rewarded for it.[65] This is so relevant to the renewal of the mind. For some people this renewal seems to happen quickly. God's power is fast at work in them and pathways shift supernaturally quickly. But even if that doesn't happen, God's power, genius design and grace is with us as we go through the process and become all the stronger for it, like the butterfly struggling to get out of its cocoon.

List three main brain pathways (triggers that turn into thoughts that lead to bad reactions) that you would like to work at rerouting with God's help.

....

....

....

List a specific truth you could use to replace each one.

....

....

....

What actions could represent the big rock you plan to use to block the bad pathway thought before it gets to the reaction stage?

....

....

....

Heading in the Right Direction

Of course, there is more than one pathway when it comes to addiction, but there are often a few main ones, and once they're dealt with the secondary ones are much easier to fix. In general, the more you close off, the easier it becomes to reroute the rest. And the more good ones you build, the easier it becomes to build further good ones.

Patience is crucial here, otherwise you will be tempted to cop out and merely conform rather than actually changing. Behaviour modification through willpower can sneak up on you, especially in recovery, and even more so if you're surrounded by people who are further on in their recovery or who have recovered fully from the same things you are battling. Genuine biblical conformity to the image of Christ and a genuine passion to be transformed can sometimes turn into acting as if you're further on than you really are. This isn't the end of the world every now and then, for short periods of time, but it will spell the end of your full recovery if you stop there and it becomes a lifestyle.

As we come to the end of this milestone, check that you're partnering with the truth (God), to be transformed, rather than conforming in your own strength through behaviour modification and willpower. Are you plucking and painting your fruit without actually changing the root?

Two guides will you help you keep yourself in check. The first is the Temptation Scale. Are you progressing through it at all? Depending on how quickly you're progressing through this workbook, you may not have made major strides yet, but it's something to keep an eye on. If you have been working hard at improving for a long time but remain stuck at points two and three on the Temptation Scale, it's likely that you're forcing behaviour modification rather than working with God to take your thoughts captive, renew your pathways and trust him to see who you really are. As we discussed before, many addicts stay at points two and three indefinitely, constantly convincing themselves that other things matter more than the one thing they want the most. They are still living under an illusion and pretending the truth has clicked, which stops them from going over it until it really does click.

The second is to think of your behaviour as the fruit of the root. If your root is changing through truthformation, it'll show in the fruit you produce. When you are being transformed by the renewing of your mind, it often looks like you're taking two steps forward and one step back, like the overcoming cravings graph in Milestone Three (Part One). Forced behaviour modification, on the other hand, often looks like sudden movements from one extreme to another: jumping back and forth from angelic behaviour and declarations of freedom from addiction to behaviour that's as bad as it has ever been, and feeling consumed by desire for the activity or substance of your addiction.

If you want to bear the right fruit, you need to change the root!

Dear God . . .

Thank you for being a genuine God who desires authenticity and honesty from me. Thank you that you are not so small and immature as to be pacified or fooled by exterior acts, but that you look at the heart and require a true transformation that is only achievable through your power.

Thank you for giving us brains that can be rewired, hearts that can be made whole and minds that can be renewed.

Thank you for the privilege and responsibility you have given me to partner with you as you do a work that only you can do in me and in my life.

I pray that you will increase my spiritual hunger for your word (the Bible) and my desire for truth, so that I may be transformed by the renewing of my mind day after day.

Please help me resist the temptation to settle for behaviour modification and pretence, either out of passion and zeal, out of a desire for acceptance and praise, or for any other reason. May I become so full of truth that I am transformed as my desires conform to your perfect desires.

Amen

You've achieved Milestone Eight!

Statement of truth:

I refuse to settle for anything less than true transformation.

'The thief comes only to steal and kill and destroy; I have come that they may have life, and have it to the full.'

John 10:10

Milestone Nine:

Out With the Lies and
In With the Truth

'The thief comes only to steal and kill and destroy; I have come that they may have life, and have it to the full.'

John 10:10

Identity

Human behaviour is borne out of our beliefs. What we believe is vitally important, and what we believe about who we are is paramount. This is true for anyone because we all have different aspects of our lives that are affected by our beliefs about ourselves, such as work, parenting and relationships, and we all love, hate, accept, reject and speak according to our beliefs. But what we believe is absolutely crucial when it comes to addiction recovery.

Think about some of the things you've done in your life and see if you can pair them up with the things you believe about yourself.

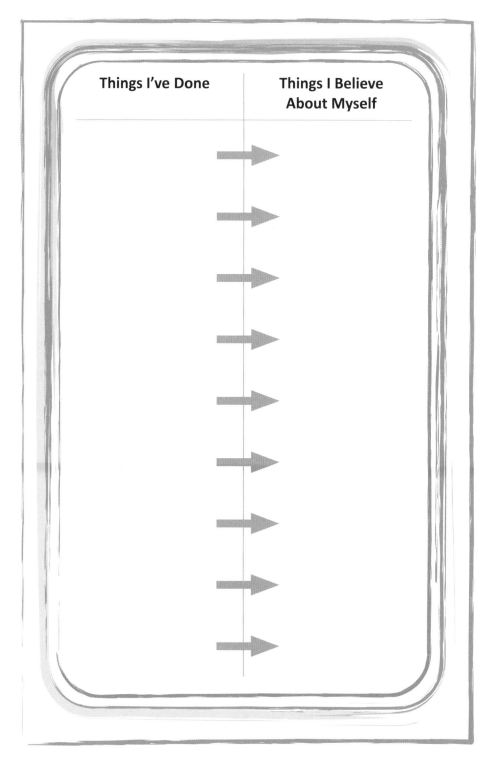

Even if we believe the truth of God's story and the truth about addiction, we will continue to go round in circles and end up in places we don't want to be if we don't believe the truth about ourselves. Perhaps that is why influential theologian John Calvin famously said: 'Without knowledge of self there is no knowledge of God.'[66] Far too many times I've seen someone grasp the truth about addiction and break free from its illusion, as well as grasping the truth of the gospel so much that they heal and grow in Christ at an amazing rate, yet they end up way off course because they still believe destructive lies about their identity. I pray this will not be the case for you!

I've met very few people who have always believed more truths about themselves than lies, because so many lies are set up against us. These lies may have been passed down from generation to generation, with one parent after another making the child feel worthless because their own parents made them feel worthless. Or maybe we're allowing media lies to crush our confidence in a bid to make us buy more of their products. Or perhaps we are still believing lies from the mouths of school bullies, which are often based on the lies they are exposed to at home.

There are so many ways these lies reach our hearts, but they all ultimately come from one place: Satan, the illusionist and enemy of our souls. And when they reach the heart, they take form in the brain. Lies about our identity are formed as pathways in our brains, so that they become ingrained and life-controlling, like a default setting. This is why someone who is really smart might think they are stupid, why someone of great value to you might think they are worthless, or why someone beautiful might think they are ugly.

Do you think these kinds of awful things about yourself? Maybe not. Maybe you think you're worthy of anything and everything good, and we'll come to that soon. Right now I'm talking to those of you who believe things about yourselves that are harsh, depressing, nasty and hurtful; things that make you feel as though you are less than other people, like you're somehow special in a negative way.

Write down all the negative things you believe about yourself in the box below.

Negative Things I Believe About Myself:

Have you ever seen a young child shrink back when they were told they were ugly, stupid or useless? Picture it now, in your mind's eye. Imagine a little girl or boy being towered over and told they are the things you've written in that box.

Do you agree with the abuser who is calling the child those things?

What would you think of someone who did that?

....

....

....

Why Do We Believe and Perpetuate the Lies?

If that's how you would feel about someone telling a child such things, and you know full well that they're wrong, why do we believe whoever it was who told *us* things like that? And why do we often do the very same things as that mean adult, by abusing ourselves?

There are two reasons why we so often believe the attacks of people whose opinions we know aren't credible, and why we then attack ourselves. The first is brain pathways (maybe you saw that one coming) and the second is trauma. Trauma is a huge topic that cannot be adequately covered here, but we're going to look into it just enough to get us on the path to rediscovering our true identity.

In addition to the general attack on identity that everyone faces, trauma can have a devastating impact. Many people in addiction have experienced trauma. Some entered into addiction with broken identity caused by trauma and others have experienced broken identity through trauma related to their addiction. Often it's both. At the end of Part One we looked at the topic of pain, and within that we faced the fact that addicts don't generally deal with pain as well as non-addicts do. Likewise, dealing with trauma is a big problem for addicts.

Trauma is a physical response that takes place in the body as well as in the soul, because the spirit, soul and body are so interconnected. Whether it's an isolated traumatic event or an ongoing traumatic experience and environment; whether it's physical damage, verbal attack, sexual abuse, emotional bereavement or suffering too complex for definition; whether it's a car accident or an abuser, it doesn't just hurt our feelings, bruise our skin and create pathways in the brain. If suffering tips over into trauma, it penetrates the person at a cellular level. It alters their DNA, even potentially being passed on to future generations.[67]

What traumatic events or situations have you experienced?

....

....

....

Now, it's important to recognise that traumatic experiences don't always lead to trauma. It's all about what follows the experience. When a traumatic experience occurs, it becomes trauma if it is not immediately replaced by a safe, healthy environment where the individual can process what has happened and allow the body to counter the physical stress reaction. I've known people go through horrendous traumatic experiences but come out the other end stronger and healthier because it took place within an environment and context conducive to processing and healing. This is why some people who were brought up in safe, loving environments cannot understand why others are so negatively affected by traumatic experiences for so long, because theirs didn't become trauma.

But in cases where abuse, neglect, dysfunctional childhood, assault, discrimination and bereavement take place within an unloving or unsafe context, the effects become ingrained. The lies we hear become beliefs. They become altered DNA. And they become brain pathways, like maps dictating where we go without us even realising it.

What do you think are the main roots of trauma in you?

....

....

....

Removing the Aluminium Bandage

Once trauma affects our very being, it becomes so dominant that everything about us is more sensitive. It's like prodding an infected wound. If you came and prodded my arm now, I'd feel it but it wouldn't hurt because my arm was fine to begin with. But if I fell and sustained a compound fracture so that the bone in my arm tore through the skin, I'd be liable to punch you, or at least push you away, if you came and prodded my arm.

Likewise, when someone is traumatised, things that wouldn't otherwise hurt are agonising. When that trauma affects their identity, implanting lies about who they are, even harmless words and actions prod the wound and make it worse. If a healthy person drops something, they pick it up. If someone with a traumatised identity drops something, it feels like a conformation that they're stupid or clumsy. If a friend is late to a coffee date with a healthy person, that person uses the time to get something done or to daydream. But if it happens to someone with a traumatised identity it feels like a confirmation that no one cares about them.

When addiction is not an issue, people can usually heal from trauma, and the quicker it happens the better. For some the healing comes entirely from God – sometimes very suddenly and sometimes from going through a process – for others therapy is a valuable resource. But for someone in addiction, none of that even touches the trauma, because addiction covers the trauma up like an aluminium bandage over the broken arm, keeping out anything that could soothe or heal it. Eventually, the wound gets infected and spreads through the rest of the body. Addiction worsens trauma.

Removing that aluminium bandage can be one of the most frightening things about addiction recovery, but the trauma will never heal while the bandage remains. It will only get worse and worse. If we believe that we are worthless, we make choices that confirm our perceived worthlessness. Likewise, when we use the aluminium bandage of addiction, trauma leads to more trauma and low self-worth leads to lower self-worth. If trauma leads us to believe that we are worthless and we don't let this heal, we will enter situations and relationships that cause further trauma. And then we will tell ourselves, 'See! I really *am* worthless!'

Have you ever noticed this pattern in your life?

Have you made any choices based on the low view you have of yourself, which ended up feeding this low view of yourself? Which examples come to mind?

....

....

....

....

....

Choosing Happiness Over Misery

When these things happen, they build additional pathways that branch out from our existing bad pathways, strengthening the lie and its control over our lives. On the other hand, when we learn, process and dwell on the truth, we are able to build new pathways that get stronger and stronger over time. We also need a big rock to put at the top of the bad pathway; something to make us stop repeating the lie and telling ourselves nasty things about who we are. Many people with chronically damaged identities have amazing breakthroughs simply by reading and speaking out statements of truth about their true identity on a regular basis. This is because they are combatting the lies with the truth and building new pathways that are more powerful than the old ones. Over time, the rainwater (triggers) follow the new watercourse (pathway) instead of the old one, leading to a good and plentiful river (positive reactions).

From what you've learned so far, what positive statements do you think God might make about you? Even if you don't believe them yet, use the box below to write down anything that comes to mind.

Good Things God Might Say About Me:

This sort of exercise really helps a lot of people, but I tried many like this and still hated myself for a long time. I constantly rejected the truth in case it wasn't true. I finally came to a point of rationality, where I figured out I'd rather believe something that didn't yet feel true but *could* be true, and that made me feel happier, than keep believing something that equally might not be true but made me miserable. It was that simple.

I also looked around me at other people who had genuine confidence and were at peace with themselves, and I noticed how attractive they were in their content authenticity. I realised they didn't really give themselves a lot of thought; they just lived life well. Then I looked around at the people who were insecure and uncomfortable with themselves and noticed how unattractive their self-hate made them. I realised how much of their attention was taken up in thinking about themselves: their flaws, their mistakes, and what others thought of their flaws and mistakes. Then I realised how much of my attention was being taken up in thinking about my own flaws and mistakes!

It was a very logical decision for me once I realised I was making myself miserable and ruining my life by stubbornly choosing to believe the bad things. It still didn't feel like I knew what was true, but I definitely knew that I wanted to choose life. Once I'd stopped rejecting the truth, it became clearer and clearer to me that the lies were lies and that the truth was truth. It took time, because changing pathways always does, even if God fast-forwards our progress a bit and gives us fresh revelation about something. But moving forward at any speed is better than staying stuck in deception and misery. Once I had chosen light over darkness, activities like the one we've just done became increasingly helpful.

Stubbed Toes

Christian leader and theologian Tim Keller suggests that having an inflated (too positive) or deflated (too negative) ego (sense of self-esteem or self-importance) is unhealthy. When we have a healthy sense of self we don't even really pay it any attention. Keller explains that it's a bit like a toe. Most people don't spend their days noticing a particular toe or thinking about it at length. But if we stub or break a toe, all our attention ends up on it![68]

Some people have unhealthy egos because they are deflated, which means they are chronically insecure and self-critical. Other people's egos are unhealthy because they are inflated, which means they are arrogant and proud. Either way, it's like a stubbed toe desperately trying to get some attention. People with healthy egos are at peace with themselves, and are focused on God, their purpose and others rather than on themselves.

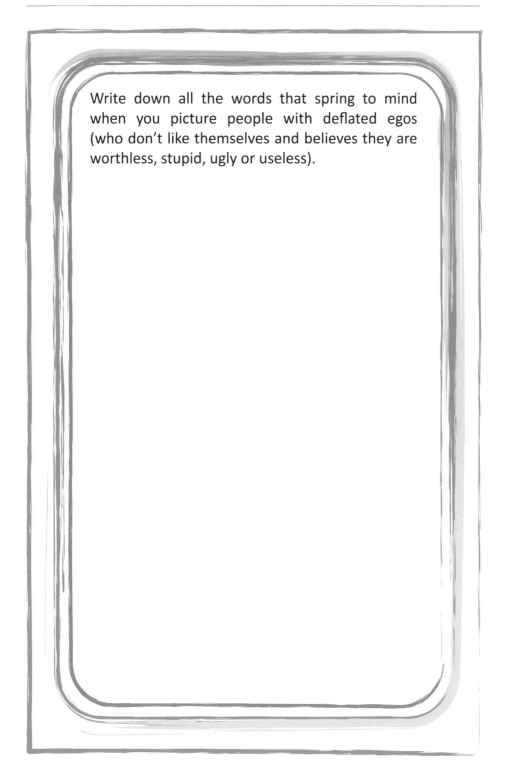

Write down all the words that spring to mind when you picture people with deflated egos (who don't like themselves and believes they are worthless, stupid, ugly or useless).

Write down all the words that come to mind when you picture people with inflated egos (who think they are flawless, superior to others and always right).

Write down all the words that come to mind when you picture those who are at peace with themselves. They are aware of their flaws and their good qualities, make the right choices to grow in their faith and are passionately focused on living a full life.

Now close your eyes and picture yourself as the last type. Truths about ourselves are formed in our brain pathways just as lies are, except that God himself is in the truth. We can create pathways that make truth our default setting, so that it is the truth that dictates our lives instead of lies.

The few people I've met who were taught the truth from a young age until it became ingrained are so blessed! They don't wrestle or struggle with the same aches and dysfunctional mindsets. But not all the people I looked at and admired had been brought up with healthy self-esteem. Many had developed it over time. And as I've said before, those of us who have had to work at cutting off the old bad pathways and at creating new, good ones usually end up being blessed by the process as well as the end result.

A Dirty Coin

So what is the truth about who you are? Picture a coin covered in so much dirt that you can't tell which country it's from, let alone work out its value. Underneath the dirt is an image, and that image makes the coin legal tender. The image remains on the coin no matter what might cover it up. The image hasn't just been engraved, etched or painted onto the coin; the metal is melted and moulded into the image as part of the coin itself. Just because you can't see the image, it doesn't mean it's not there.

Even when Adam and Eve were banished from paradise, the image of God never left humanity because he made us 'in his image'.[69] It is this image that validates our core value. Without the work Jesus did on earth and the ongoing work of the Holy Spirit, we become so covered in dirt that the image is hardly visible, if it is visible at all. But we all bear that image whether we can see it or not.

When a pesky bunch of people tried to trap Jesus with a question about taxes under corrupt Roman rule, Jesus turned their trick on its head by turning their attention to the image on the coin. He asked them whose image it was, and they correctly answered that it was Caesar's. 'Then Jesus said to them, "Give back to Caesar what is Caesar's and to God what is God's." And they were amazed at him.'[70] He was saying the value of the coin came from the image on it, and therefore the coin belonged to Caesar. But he was also referring to the image of God in humanity.

Jesus' Jewish audience would have known what he meant because the scriptures played an important part in their lives, and they knew that God had created humanity in his image. It also applies to us as born-again believers, because in the same way that a coin has an image in it, we have God's image in us. This image declares *his* authority and *our* value. Whatever wounds, baggage, shame and sin we carry, that image is still there underneath it all, ingrained and immovable.

Being saved, transformed, sanctified, healed and starting to grow isn't about changing who we are as people. It is about restoring God's image on and in us by removing all the muck of false belief, shame, wounds, distractions, angst, distorted love, evil desires and of general godlessness that leads to destructive behaviours, bad attitudes and dysfunctional relationships, and that pulls us away from him. God loves your sense of humour, your personality, your quirks, your talents, your idiosyncrasies and the things that make you who you really are; He designed you himself![71] He doesn't want you to be like a robot. He wants you to be unique and diverse, but a Christlike version of yourself that isn't so covered in muck it covers up his image on and in you.

Which parts of your personality do you think God designed on purpose when you were knitted together and formed in your mother's womb?

....

....

....

Which unique and special parts of yourself do you remember from childhood, which have since been covered up and hidden by the muck of sin and death in your life? (You may need to ask God to remind you of these things.)

....

....

....

Being a Christian isn't about acting like a good person. It's about developing a relationship with your Creator, worshipping him instead of substitute gods (such as money, drugs, social media, self or another person), and gradually being made more like the person he intended you to be as you partner with him and allow his power (the Holy Spirit) to work in you. He wants you to be your true self, without all the corruption, damage, emptiness, angst, selfishness, self-consciousness, unease, trauma, false beliefs, evil desires and dysfunction.

Because I'm Worth It

Another way to understand what we're *worth* is to consider how *unworthy* we are. We are of indescribable value, yet not deserving. If Jesus had paid a price we deserved – if we'd earned it somehow – it wouldn't have required his love to pay it. We are worth such an incredible amount to God that Jesus died for us even when we were totally unworthy of it!

If we remove God from therapy that deals with low self-esteem, the only remaining option is to convince each other that we are innately worthy. This doesn't work, because we're not.

'This is Me', a song from *The Greatest Showman*, became really popular – and for good reason. It's a powerful song! But there's a line in it that people might sing to make themselves feel better which simply isn't true. The line declares the singer's infinite worthiness of anything and everything.

After the song's release, quite a few people I was pastoring with low self-esteem said the song had become their anthem, but others were quick to see that it was flawed because we're not actually worthy of anything good. No matter how catchy and motivational a song is, those who know the God story know that we're not worthy, and many others know it instinctively. Depending how much we've pushed it down or how much narcissism has taken hold, there's still a voice of truth within us that knows we aren't truly worthy of anything as we lay our heads on our pillows at night.

We're not *worthy* of much at all – in fact what we're actually worthy of is punishment. But we are *worth it*! To God we are so valuable that he has given us the salvation, blessing and intimacy we could never have earned based on our own merit.

Do you remember looking at redemption in Milestone Six? Jesus paid the highest price possible to buy you back – to redeem you – from captivity. That's how much you're *worth* to him. But if you had already been *worthy*, he wouldn't have needed to pay the price he paid. Therefore, it is precisely because we are not worthy that we can understand our incredible worth to God! The Bible puts it like this: 'Very rarely will anyone die for a righteous person, though for a good person someone might possibly dare to die. But God demonstrates his own love for us in this: While we were still sinners, Christ died for us.'[72] If we had deserved Jesus' sacrifice, he would have died out a sense of duty, but we know that he died despite the fact we weren't worthy to demonstrate his incredible love.

While it's obvious that children bought up in ways that made them feel worthless would likely grow into adults with low self-worth, they're not the only ones. Children who are bought up in high-achieving environments – in which they experience a lot of praise for how good they are at things – often become adults with very low self-esteem because they don't understand that they are loved and valued for who they are, regardless of what they do. All their self-worth is tied up in being worthy, and they know that the standards are too high because deep down we all know that we're unworthy.

Were you brought up to feel worthless? Or brought up feeling like you had to prove yourself worthy of the love you were given through your actions and success? Or maybe you were brought up with healthy self-esteem but life (or addiction, perhaps) knocked it out of you. Share your experience here.

....

....

....

The Older Brother's Problem

Jesus once told a story of two sons. The younger brother requested his inheritance early (a shockingly shameful thing to do in that time and culture). He left his family's land and went off to spend his dad's money. He cast off all restraint, painted the town red, had a wild one and tried everything going until he was spent and poor. He ended up taking the only work he could find to survive, feeding pigs. And he was so hungry he ate their food. This was rock bottom for a person in that culture, where pigs were seen as the lowest of the low. It was at that point, while eating pig swill, that the Bible says he 'came to his senses'.[73]

Having done so, the young man prepared to confess to his father that he was 'no longer worthy' to be his son. He had to realise exactly how unworthy he was before he could restore the relationship. He returned to his father's house with his tail between his legs, hoping he'd be shown enough favour to work as a servant in his father's house. That was when he discovered his true worth! The father ran out to meet him, then pulled out all the stops to celebrate his return. He didn't do this because the son had done anything to deserve it. He simply did it because his son was of great worth to him.

Do you feel like you've 'come to your senses' and realised how unworthy you are? What does it tell you about Father God's love for you to know that Jesus died to buy your salvation, freedom and relationship with him?

....

....

....

When the older son saw the way the father had reacted to his younger brother's return, he was full of resentment. He was angry. The older son felt he was worthy of the treatment the younger son was receiving, and that the younger son wasn't. The older son had worked so hard and made such an effort that he thought he was worthy of his dad's love. He didn't realise how much he was worth just because of who he was. He complained to the father that, despite all his good behaviour, he'd never received what the brother was now receiving, despite all his bad behaviour. But the father told him, 'Everything I have is yours.'[74] The older brother felt rejected because he was so focused on trying to be worthy that he couldn't see how much he was really worth.

What efforts have you made in your life to become worthy?

....

....

Have you ever been like the older brother, comparing and judging how loved you are based on who gets what because you didn't know your true value? How did that feel?

....

....

....

There is also an incredible next level of truth to our unworthiness and worth. Not only did Jesus pay the highest possible price to redeem us because we are worth it to him – despite our unworthiness – but through his sacrifice he actually made us worthy. He gave us *his* worthiness! He clothes us in *his* righteousness.[75] His worthiness is bestowed on us.

So, having realised your innate worth by accepting your unworthiness and the price he paid without you doing anything to deserve it, you have become worthy through the worthiness of God within you. Everything will change for the better if you can grasp this, but it takes some longer than others. My husband used to amaze me with his confident grasp on this truth, while I got it much more gradually. I'm still learning to get it, actually, but the more I do, the better life gets. Grasping this reality is crucial to true recovery, and in my experience it is the truth Satan the illusionist is most against us grasping because he knows we remain vulnerable to his tricks so long as we don't know our worth, but that we become unstoppable in recovery if we do.

Dear God . . .

Thank you for making me in your image and for being able and willing to remove all the muck that has covered up your image within me for so long.

Thank you for placing such a high value on me that you deemed me worth paying the highest possible price for, even though I wasn't worthy.

I pray that you will miraculously remove any lies about myself from my being if it is your will, but if it is your will that I dismantle them over time, I thank you for the strength and blessing that will create as I go through the process.

In faith, I choose to believe what you say about me, even if I don't feel it yet. Please help the truth about my identity in you to become more than mere head knowledge. I pray that it would become heart revelation. In the meantime, I choose to believe by faith.

Please help me to stick to you as my one true source of identity.

Amen

You've achieved Milestone Nine!

Statement of truth:

I choose to increasingly believe what is true about myself and reject the lies.

'The thief comes only to steal and kill and destroy; I have come that they may have life, and have it to the full.'

John 10:10

Twelve Statements of Truth

1. I realise and accept that my choices, behaviour and feelings have been influenced by a con, and that I can break free from it by knowing and understanding how the con works.

2. I realise that addiction is a type of brain damage, but that God gave my brain the ability to heal when his amazing design is hijacked.

3. I recognise that a craving is the feeling caused by faulty brain activity, and a vicious cycle in which every use makes me need the next use. I understand that using continues the craving, while not using stops it.

4. I will be free from all wrong desire once I have truly understood that addiction is a trick and know how it works. In the meantime, I will exercise willpower as a temporary means.

5. I accept that some pain is useful, some pain is necessary and some pain brings healing. I determine to let pain do its job in my recovery and life.

6. I recognise that an enemy provides false relief, but God sacrificed himself to provide true freedom.

7. I accept and appreciate the struggles and joys of process for all the good it can produce in me.

8. I refuse to settle for anything less than true transformation.

9. I choose to increasingly believe what is true about myself and reject the lies.

10. I recognise God's holiness and my sin. I choose to approach God in repentance, which I can only do because Jesus made a way for me to become pure through his own sacrifice. I recognise that God loves me, so I don't need to live in shame but can continue to be sanctified by his Holy Spirit, who lives in me.

11. I consciously decide to forgive the wrongs committed against me, and I accept God's forgiveness for all the wrongs I have done.

12. I seek to make amends where I am responsible and put things right where possible, in the full confidence that Jesus has righted my wrongs spiritually and eternally, and will one day right all wrongs.

Endnotes

Milestone 6

1. John 7:37–38.

2. Romans 3:23; Ephesians 2:1–5.

3. Genesis 1; 26.

4. Genesis 2:7–25.

5. Genesis 2:7.

6. Genesis 2:18–23.

7. 'ezer', Bible Hub: https://biblehub.com/hebrew/5828.htm and 'Helper: defining the ezer woman, Hebrew Word Lessons :https://hebrewwordlessons.com/2018/05/13/helper-defining-the-ezer-woman (both accessed 3 August 2022).

8. From the start of the Bible, right through to the end, it's clear that God's desire has always been to create an environment without sin, suffering and tears. See Genesis 1; Luke 23:43; Revelation 21:1-4 for more on this.

9. Genesis 2:15–17; 3:6–7.

10. Romans 3:9; 7:14–20; 8:2; Galatians 5:1.

11. 1 John 4:4; 5:19.

12. Genesis 3:22–24.

13. Ecclesiastes 3:11.

14. John 3:19.

15. Isaiah 61:8; Psalms 5:4; 7:11; Proverbs 6:16–19; John 3:16; Hebrews 1:9; 1 John 4:10.

16. My own version of Leviticus 24:19–21.

17. 2 Corinthians 5:18–9.

18. Exodus 26:31–5.

19. 2 Peter 3:8–9.

20. Proverbs 4:19.

21. See Romans 9:30-32, John 3:16 and Ephesians 2:8 for more on this.

22. 1 Peter 1:18–20; Revelation 13:8.

23. Genesis 3:15.

24. 'How many prophecies did Jesus fulfill?' Got Questions: https://www.gotquestions.org/prophecies-of-Jesus.html (accessed 3 August 2022).

25. Isaiah 9:6; Micah 5:2.

26. Matthew 5:17.

27. See John 1:1–18 (MSG).

28. For more on Jesus' blood, see Matthew 26:28 and 27:24; Luke 22:44; John 19:34.

29. Hebrews 1:3.

30. Matthew 5:38–40.

31. Matthew 23:27–28.

32. Isaiah 64:6; John 3:16; Romans 3:23; 6:23.

33. Max Lucado, *He Chose the Nails* (W Publishing Group: 2000), pp. 95–96.

34. Matthew 27:51–52.

35. Romans 5:8.

36. 1 Corinthians 15:3–8.

37. John 14:18, Hebrews 10:11–14.

38. John 17:4

39. John 19:30.

40. Acts 9:2; 19:9, 23; 22:4; 24:14, 22.

41. John 3:3, 7; 1 Corinthians 6:19–20; 1 Peter 1:23.

42. John 3:3–8.

43. 2 Corinthians 5:21.

44. Romans 8:14–19.

45. Galatians 5:22–3.

46. 2 Corinthians 3:18.

47. Matthew 16:18.

48. 'Ecclesia', britannica.com: https://www.britannica.com/topic/Ecclesia-ancient-Greek-assembly (accessed 11 August 2022).

49. 1 Samuel 8:19–21.

50. 1 Corinthians 12:27.

51. Revelation 22:1–2.

52. Revelation 21: 1–5.

53. John 1:12.

54. John 10:10.

55. John Mark Comer, *Live No Lies* (Form Publishing: 2021) pp. 18–21.

56. John 8:32.

57. Neil T. Anderson and Steve Goss, *Freedom in Christ: Participant's guide* (Lion Hudson Limited: 2017), pp. 83-84.

Milestone 8

58 '4832. summorphos', Bible Hub: https://biblehub.com/greek/4832.htm (accessed 4 August 2022).

59 '4964. suschématizó', Bible Hub: https://biblehub.com/greek/4964.htm (accessed 4 August 2022).

60 Christine Comaford, 'Got Inner Peace? 5 Ways To Get It Now', Forbes: https://www.forbes.com/sites/christinecomaford/2012/04/04/got-inner-peace-5-ways-to-get-it-now/?sh=45af5e906672; Magsud Rahmanov, '80% of Our Thoughts Are Negative – Control Them!' LinkedIn: https://www.linkedin.com/pulse/80-our-thoughts-negative-control-them-magsud-rahmanov (both accessed 4 August 2022).

61 Caroline Leaf, *Who Switched Off my Brain?* (Thomas Nelson: 2009, Revised Edition), pp. 13–17.

62 John Andrews, *Truthformation* (ESB Resources: 2003), pp. 5–6.

63 2 Corinthians 10:5.

64 Philippians 4:8.

65 Galatians 6:9.

Milestone 9

66 John Calvin, 'Institutes of the Christian Religion (I.1.i)', CRTA: https://reformed.org/books/institutes/books/book1/bk1ch01.html (accessed 5 August 2022).

67 Roberto Colangeli, 'Bound Together: How Psychoanalysis Diminishes Inter-generational DNA Trauma' in *The American Journal of Psychoanalysis 80* (2020), pp. 196–218.

68 Tim Keller, *The Freedom of Self-Forgetfulness* (10Publishing: 2012), pp. 15–17.

69 Genesis 1:27.

70 Mark 12:17.

71 Psalms 139:13–14.

72 Romans 5:7–8.

73 Luke 15:17–20.

74 Luke 15:31.

75 Isaiah 61:10.